Empowered
for
Purpose

Books by Linda Evans Shepherd

Empowered
for
Purpose

Winning Your Daily Spiritual Battles

Linda Evans Shepherd

SPIRE

© 2016 by Linda Evans Shepherd

Published by Revell
a division of Baker Publishing Group
PO Box 6287, Grand Rapids, MI 49516-6287
www.revellbooks.com

Spire edition published 2020
ISBN 978-0-8007-3831-0

Previously published in 2016 as *Winning Your Daily Spiritual Battles*

Printed in the United States of America

Published in association with the Books & Such Literary Agency, 52 Mission Circle, Suite 122, PMB 170, Santa Rosa, CA 95409-7953.

20 21 22 23 24 25 26   7 6 5 4 3 2 1

To my dear husband, Paul

God has been our constant help and companion through our many life adventures. I'm so glad we share this journey together.

Contents

Acknowledgments

A special thanks to Team Revell and my wonderful editor Vicki Crumpton. Also a special thanks to my agent, Janet Grant, and my dedicated prayer team. I so appreciate you all.

Introduction

> For we are God's masterpiece. He has created us anew in
> Christ Jesus, so we can do the good things he planned for
> us long ago.
>
> Ephesians 2:10 NLT

I opened my eyes and stared into the darkness. Was someone calling my name?

I threw back my covers and bolted to my daughter's room. I found Laura in her bed, pale and unable to breathe. Soon my driveway glowed with the rotating lights of a fire truck and ambulance as emergency workers hurried to whisk my disabled child to the hospital.

After they admitted Laura into the ICU with a life-threatening pneumonia, I stood by her side and prayed over her until morning when a friend arrived so I could go home to rest. But when I laid my head on my pillow, it was as if the last twenty-seven years of my life melted into a single moment of shock.

In my dream life, I was once again crawling out of the broken window of the smashed car. I was once again running down the freeway searching for my baby in the aftermath of the car crash. I was once again feeling the shock of finding my baby in her car seat in the middle of the freeway. It took only one look and I knew. My baby had been changed—forever.

My heart pounded me awake, and the realization hit me hard. After all these years, my daughter was once again in the ICU fighting for her life.

I pressed my tears into the covers and prayed the most powerful prayer I knew: "Lord, please hide my daughter in you. Hide her from the one who would take her life. I put her into your armor: your helmet of salvation, your breastplate of righteousness, your belt of truth. I put Laura into the shoes of the gospel of peace and cover her with your shield of faith, which will deflect all the arrows of the enemy. I take up the sword of the Spirit, which is your Word made alive in your Spirit, and I pray for her life. Lord, my daughter belongs to you, but I cannot help but ask, Could you once again spare her life?"

God heard and answered my prayer, and though Laura's life hung in the balance for several days, she was released from the hospital and is continuing to do well. Praise God!

The prayer I prayed for my daughter illustrates the incredible secret of this book, the secret of how to pray with God's empowerment for protection, victory, and purpose through the armor of God. But before I begin to unwrap this secret of how to win your daily spiritual battles, I want to ask you an important question. Have you ever been surprised when something in your life went wrong?

So have I.

I mean, if God really loves us, why do we face trouble? Is there something we are missing? An important secret that would help us have victory over our trials?

It is hard to believe now, but when I was a child, I somehow lived in a protective bubble, sheltered from the horrors of tragedies, hate, and difficulties. But bubbles can only float so far before they burst. When they do, they evaporate into thin air as if they never existed.

I was fifteen when my world exploded with the news of the death of my twelve-year-old cousin from a brain aneurism. The funeral was on my sixteenth birthday. I sat in the church pew with my family and wondered why God hadn't protected my cousin from death. I also wondered why we, her family, were left with her memory instead of the child herself. Sure, I knew she was in heaven, but how I wanted her to be with us on Earth. Didn't God care that we were all heartbroken? I listened as my family sang the chorus to that old hymn:

> In the sweet by and by,
> We shall meet on that beautiful shore.[1]

I couldn't help but wonder, *The by and by is fine, I guess, but where is God in the now?*

Perhaps, like me, somewhere during the story of your life, you too had that moment when you questioned why your life journey contained some pretty rough passages. Maybe you wondered why a loving God allowed your sorrow and heartache. Or why you were hindered when you tried to do something to honor God.

Perhaps the answer to why trials happen can be found in this quotation from author Rick Stedman, who cuts to the chase: "Life is difficult because we have an incredibly malicious, and highly organized, persistent, and darkly devious enemy who is out to destroy us."[2]

Only when we understand that we have an enemy can we begin to understand how to defeat him. Author Susie Larson once explained, "Jesus came to give us *life*. Satan came to steal it from us, to kill our dreams and our passion, and destroy every hint of God-inspired sparkle or verve within us."[3] The apostle Paul wrote in his second letter to the church of Corinth, "I don't want Satan to outwit us. After all, we are not ignorant about Satan's scheming" (2 Cor. 2:11 GW).

Or are we?

I have to admit I was so ignorant about the existence of spiritual warfare that I actually held the door open for a number of devastating attacks of the enemy. Maybe you have too. In the pages of this book, I will show you how to lock the door against preventable attacks and how to wear the spiritual armor God has provided to help you win your spiritual battles so you can live into your purpose.

To be honest, it wasn't until I was in college and spent a summer leading Vacation Bible Schools around the state of Texas that I stumbled upon a truth that opened my eyes. The more difficulties my ministry partner, nineteen-year-old Lilly, and I had at the start of each new VBS, the more children came to faith in God at the end of the week. Lilly and I discussed this amazing correlation. The enemy knew God was going to move big-time, so we faced lost luggage, misunderstandings, and other ministry hazards. It got to the point that when difficulties challenged us, we would look at each other and grin. "This is going to be a great week!"

But still, we didn't know the secret of how to win our daily spiritual battles. I'm talking about the same kind of battles the enemy wages against every believer, the battles over our God-given destinies and purposes.

Let's get on the same page and agree that we will no longer cling to our bubble illusions. There is a battle, as Jesus explained in Matthew 11:12, "And from the days of John the Baptist until now the kingdom of heaven suffers violence, and the violent take it by force" (NKJV). And we must know how to fight.

In the pages of this book, you will enjoy a continuing allegory of Mezana, a former slave girl, as she discovers the secrets of how to win the battle for purpose. And you will learn how you can win the battle for your life and purpose. You will discover Paul's teaching on the armor of God and learn how to use these truths yourself. You will follow Paul's journeys to gain insights into your own battles. You will pray powerful prayers to help lead you to every victory God has in mind for you.

If you're ready to win every spiritual battle, turn the page.

1

Our Quest for Purpose

I cry out to God Most High,
   to God who will fulfill his purpose for me.

Psalm 57:2 NLT

In Louis L'Amour's story "Trap of Gold," a prospector named Wetherton follows a sprinkling of gold dust through a sandy desert to a vein of quartz laced with gold nuggets. The only trouble is that the vein runs across the base of a three-hundred-foot tower of rock, ready to crumble on anyone who dares to take a pickax to it. But with care, Wetherton is able to dig a finger deep into the crumbly quartz and pull out several gold nuggets. Holding the yellow metal in his hand, he considers the risk of digging out the rich vein. He knows the dig is a certain death trap. If the tower of rock falls on him, no one will ever find him, much less recover his gold.

I think many of us can identify with Wetherton. We want to buy into the world's lies of happiness and riches while hoping we're not trading our lives for the sake of fool's gold.

For Wetherton, the temptation of the gold is more than he can bear. Day after day he lies on his back, breaking the gold free from the quartz as he pushes his body deeper into the notch he carved at the foot of the rock tower, all the while waiting for it to tumble on him like a felled tree. L'Amour wrote, "As if to tantalize him into working on and on, the deeper he cut the richer the ore became. By nightfall of that day he had taken out more than a thousand dollars. Now the lust of the gold was getting into him, taking him by the throat. . . . Three more days to go—could he leave it then?"[1]

As with Wetherton, the more we try to gain all the world has to offer, the more likely we will dig ourselves a hole that could become our own grave.

How do we escape these worldly traps, the enslavements that our enemy Satan, the king of this world, uses to capture our hearts, minds, and souls? Truth be told, we can do so only through the power of Christ Jesus.

Our escape route is recorded in Jesus's own words when he stood up in the synagogue to read the Scriptures. He unrolled the scroll of Isaiah and read:

> The Spirit of the LORD is upon me,
>   for he has anointed me to bring Good News to
>   the poor.
> He has sent me to proclaim that captives will be
>   released,
>   that the blind will see,

> that the oppressed will be set free,
> and that the time of the Lord's favor has come.
> (Luke 4:18–19 NLT)

Jesus returned the scroll and explained, "The Scripture you've just heard has been fulfilled this very day!" (Luke 4:21 NLT). Jesus provided our escape route through his death on the cross. He allowed his own blood to be shed so he could be our sacrificial lamb, the lamb slain for the forgiveness of sin.

But thanks be to God, Jesus did not remain in the grave. On the third day he rose to life, defeating both sin and death. And in so doing, Jesus, God's only begotten Son, set the captives free (Eph. 4:8).

Jesus laid down his life for us for several reasons, including:

- his great love for us
- to forgive us of our sins
- to free us from the captivity of this world
- to give us purpose

"To give us purpose" is exactly the point Zechariah, the high priest of Jerusalem, prophesied about our Messiah: "We have been rescued from our enemies so we can serve God without fear, in holiness and righteousness for as long as we live" (Luke 1:74–75 NLT).

Our Quest

God has a purpose in mind for each of us, and Charles Stanley said, "He wants us to discover it and live in the middle of it."[2] That seems like a lovely goal, but is it even possible? Does God write his purposes for us on the clouds so we might clearly understand them?

Actually, God writes his purposes for us on our hearts. Though we may not have the whole picture at any given time, that's okay. Stanley explains, "At times He may reveal to us a portion of His will. We may know that God has brought us to a certain point but not know all that is connected with being there. Remember, Abraham did not wait for God's promise to be completely revealed to him before he obeyed the Lord. Instead he left his home believing in the One who had called him."[3] We are called to follow God's direction for our lives as best we can. It's while we are on the way that our callings become clearer.

Imagine you are lost in the woods on a dark night, unsure of where to place your next step. What if you pulled a small penlight out of your pocket and flicked it on? That tiny beam of light could be enough to help you move forward one step at a time. This is exactly how Jesus directs us. He said in John 8:12, "I am the light of the world. If you follow me, you won't have to walk in darkness, because you will have the light that leads to life" (NLT).

All you have to do to find your purpose is to be willing to walk with him, then to take that next step as soon as it presents itself. To follow the light to your purpose, try praying:

Dear Lord,

Be my light! Please rescue me from the lies of Satan. Rescue me through the escape you provided for me through the death and resurrection of your Son, Jesus. I receive his gift of sacrifice and salvation, and in exchange I give you

my life. Thank you for your gift of love, your forgiveness,
your freedom from captivity, and your purpose for my life.
Teach me how to follow you so that the great deceiver does
not steal the plans you have for me. In Jesus's name, amen.

Mezana's Quest

To help you understand the importance of your quest for
purpose, I want to tell you a story. You were a slave to sin
but were redeemed through the blood of Christ. And so the
story goes with our heroine, Mezana.

Mezana was a beauty, her silky hair cascading down her
embroidered robes of cobalt blue. She was her father's favorite daughter, born of love and laughter. She was only a
child when her father's tents were raided by slavers. She tried
to fight off her attackers, but they dragged her back to their
camp a prisoner, to do with whatever they willed.

The desert didn't stop her from trying to escape, but each
time she tried to run, her captors found her and beat her
mercilessly. There was no one to rescue her. No one to tell her
she was loved and beautiful. No one to wipe away her tears.
No one who even remembered her name. She was called
"Stupid!" "Trash!" "Ugly!" "Worthless!"

Her beauty was traded for scars, the mark of a whip in the
hand of a cruel master. Her hair was short and matted, her
clothes were rags, and she knew her life was barely worth the rotting scraps thrown from her captors' table. Soiled and broken,
she was no longer worthy of belonging to her father's house.

It seemed that she'd once had a purpose. But all that had
been forgotten, that is, until the day a prince named Asriel

showed up at the camp to rescue her. She'd never met this prince before, but he looked at her with such love and compassion that she had to hide her tears. What amazed her most was that the prince was bargaining with her captors for her freedom.

"Why should we give her to you?" her captors demanded.

"My father sent me," Asriel explained.

"But she is worthless."

"Not to my father."

"What will you give us for her, for we trade only in human life?"

"Then I will give myself."

The slavers howled with laughter. "Sold! You have foolishly fallen into our trap and now belong to our master, the evil one. Neither you nor the girl will ever leave here alive."

With those words, the slavers fell upon Asriel and beat him, leaving him for dead. Mezana wept and for her tears was locked inside her filthy cell.

"No one will rescue you now," her captors sneered. "You belong to us until you rot."

Three days later, much to her shock, Asriel peered into her cell. He smiled and opened her prison door with a key. "Come with me," he told her. "I have bought you at a terrible price. You are free to go."

The Allegory Explained

The story of Mezana and Asriel (a name meaning "Prince of God") should sound familiar, for it is of course an allegorical telling of what Christ did for us. This allegory is not meant to be a counterfeit gospel but a representation of that old, old story, the story in which the Prince of heaven, God's own Son, came down to Earth to rescue us from our captor, Satan. It was Satan who kidnapped us for his kingdom of darkness, and it wasn't until Jesus traded his life for ours, defeating sin and death by rising from the dead, that we were set free from the enemy of this world.

And we are free—free to follow Christ and to do all that he's called us to do. Most of us would gladly obey his call, except for one thing: the evil one is still the enemy of our souls. He tries to torment us, he lies and confuses us, and he sets up roadblocks to prevent us from doing the will of our Father. Lysa TerKeurst explains, "In reaching out to others with the love of Christ, you will encounter great opposition. Satan will do all he can to discourage and defeat you."[4] The apostle Peter understood this and warned, "Stay alert! Watch out for your great enemy, the devil. He prowls around like a roaring lion, looking for someone to devour" (1 Pet. 5:8 NLT).

So following Christ comes with a warning to "Stay alert!" and to "Watch out!" as we follow our God-given purposes. In the coming chapters, we will learn how to put on the whole armor of God so we can stand against our enemy and even defeat his schemes. Then we can accomplish all that God himself has called us to do.

Meet the Man Who Would Become the Apostle Paul

Paul, whose letters make up at least thirteen books of the Bible, is one of our best teachers on how to live the Christian life and how to have victory over our enemy. However, Paul was not one of the original twelve disciples. So who was he?

Paul was originally called Saul of Tarsus, a man born in a God-fearing family living in Turkey. At thirteen, Saul was sent to Jerusalem to study under a prominent Pharisee, Rabbi Gamaliel. Afterward, he studied the law, hoping to become a member of the Sanhedrin, the Jewish Supreme Court.

Saul was likely in Jerusalem during the time of Jesus's earthly ministry. Perhaps he stood in the crowd with the Pharisees when they tested Jesus with their trick questions. Maybe he was there the day Jesus cast out an evil spirit from a man who was instantly healed from being both blind and dumb. The Pharisees scoffed, "This man can force demons out of people only with the help of Beelzebul, the ruler of demons" (Matt. 12:24 GW).

But Jesus told them, "Every kingdom divided against itself is ruined. And every city or household divided against itself will not last. If Satan forces Satan out, he is divided against himself. How, then, can his kingdom last? If I force demons out of people with the help of Beelzebul, who helps your followers force them out?" (Matt. 12:25–27 GW).

Seeds of anger may have been planted in Saul's heart when Jesus went on to scold his role models, saying, "You poisonous snakes! How can you evil people say anything good? Your mouth says what comes from inside you. Good people do the good things that are in them. But evil people do the evil things that are in them" (Matt. 12:34–35 GW).

With all this going on, there's no doubt Saul was aware of Jesus and who he claimed to be. More than likely, Saul's great hope was that Jesus's death on the cross would end his controversial claim that he was the Messiah. But when

Christ's followers declared that Jesus had been raised from the dead, Saul was no doubt outraged. Would this Jesus nightmare ever end?

We know Saul's anger toward the followers of Jesus was building. In fact, following the crucifixion of Christ, young Saul was present at the stoning of Stephen. In the moments before the first stone was hurled, Saul heard Stephen describe how the Jewish people had killed their own prophets. Stephen ended his message by telling the Pharisees:

> How stubborn can you be? How can you be so heartless and disobedient? You're just like your ancestors. They always opposed the Holy Spirit, and so do you! Was there ever a prophet your ancestors didn't persecute? They killed those who predicted that a man with God's approval would come. You have now become the people who betrayed and murdered that man. You are the people who received Moses' Teachings, which were put into effect by angels. But you haven't obeyed those teachings. (Acts 7:51–53 GW)

These words of Stephen condemned Saul and his peers and, ironically, condemned Stephen to death by their hand.

Moments after Stephen's speech, Saul was found holding the coats of those who hurled stones at Stephen. As Saul watched Stephen die, his heart hardened with Stephen's last words: "Lord, don't hold this sin against them" (Acts 7:60 GW).

Sin? Saul must have thought. *This man's death by our hand is no sin. My friends and I are doing God a favor.*

In the days that followed, Saul became so zealous against the Christians that he became known as a religious terrorist, dragging Christians from their homes, arresting them, and tossing them into jail.

So how could it be that this Saul would be the very man Jesus would call to become his apostle? How did Saul change from Christ's chief persecutor to Christ's chief spokesman? How did he go from throwing Christians into jail to writing the following words to the church at Colossae: "And now, just as you accepted Christ Jesus as your Lord, you must continue to follow him. Let your roots grow down into him, and let your lives be built on him. Then your faith will grow strong in the truth you were taught, and you will overflow with thankfulness" (Col. 2:6–7 NLT)?

We will learn more about Saul's journey as well as his powerful teachings in the coming chapters.

The Armor

Paul, formerly Saul, penned the famous Ephesians 6 passage about the armor of God, a passage we will soon study at length.

But for now it's interesting to note that the apostle Paul was not the first one to describe the armor of God. It was the prophet Isaiah who first described our Redeemer wearing armor. In this passage, God is not pleased that haters came against his people. Isaiah said:

> He saw and wondered that there was no man to speak up for what is right. Then His own arm brought saving power, and what is right with Him gave Him strength. Being right and good was His covering for His breast, saving power was His headcovering, clothing of anger was his covering, and His strong desires were like a coat. (Isa. 59:16–17 NLV)

This passage continues to declare God's anger toward and punishment of those who hate him and his people. But then Isaiah stops to say something that makes my heart leap with joy: "'And as for Me, this is My agreement with them,' says the Lord. 'My Spirit which is upon you, and My Words which I have put in your mouth, will not leave your mouth, or the mouth of your children, or the mouth of your children's children,' says the Lord, 'from now and forever'" (Isa. 59:21 NLV).

What a wonderful promise. As we realize that God's armor and Spirit are available for us today, we see that we have nothing to fear from the enemy. As Psalm 91 exclaims:

> He will cover you with his feathers.
>> He will shelter you with his wings.
>> His faithful promises are your armor and
>>> protection.
> Do not be afraid of the terrors of the night,
>> nor the arrow that flies in the day.
> Do not dread the disease that stalks in darkness,
>> nor the disaster that strikes at midday.
> Though a thousand fall at your side,
>> though ten thousand are dying around you,
>> these evils will not touch you. (vv. 4–7 NLT)

Suiting Up

Strongholds are like bridges the enemy has legal authority to cross. But through prayer, we can close and even destroy those bridges.

Recently, I was praying with a friend. "What do you believe about your current troubles?" I asked her.

"I believe I deserve my difficulties. I'm stupid. I've made some bad decisions in my past, and so now the enemy has the right to torment me. My failures are exactly what I deserve."

I was shocked by Karen's words. "You're believing a lie," I explained. "You don't have to live in defeat and failure; you can live in victory. You have the power to cancel these lies and put them under the blood of Jesus. Would you like to do that?"

"Yes, I really would."

Karen and I prayed that God would destroy this stronghold, namely, the enemy's lie that he had the right to torment her. We also prayed that God would take her failures and turn them into victory, not because she deserved it but because she was appealing to God through Christ, her Redeemer.

At the end of the prayer, Karen said, "The lies I believed have been broken. I now feel that God can and will answer my prayers. I finally realize I'm not praying in my own righteousness. I am praying in the righteousness of Christ."

Dear Lord,

Help me to realize that you see me through the lens of the righteousness of Jesus. Help me to believe that you love me and want good things for me. Teach me how to live and to walk by faith, defeating the attacks of the enemy that come against me. In Jesus's name, amen.

ARMORED RESPONSE

To help you break free from the enemy's assignments, I want to show you how to put on the power of God's promises, which you can declare (aloud, please) over your circumstances. This declaration will build your faith as it gives you permission to believe in the power of God over your struggle. Watch for these armored promises and prayers to set you free at the end of each chapter.

Failure-Fighting Scripture

"It is God who arms me with strength, and makes my way perfect" (Ps. 18:32 NKJV).

Declaration to Defeat Failure

I declare that God arms me with his strength and makes my way perfect. I declare the Lord's victory over me.

Prayer for Victory over Failure

Dear Lord,

Forgive me for allowing the spirit of defeat to rule my heart. I thank you for defeating the spirit of failure over me. I cancel the assignment of the spirit of defeat and nail this assignment to the cross, erasing it from my life. I ask you, Lord, to gift me with your victory through the power of the name and the blood of Jesus and through the empowerment of God's Holy Spirit. Amen.

2

Who Are You Wearing?

Put on your new nature, created to be like God—truly righteous and holy.

Ephesians 4:24 NLT

When you look into the mirror, do you see yourself as God describes you, with a holy and righteous nature? Or do you see yourself as the person the enemy says you are, pitiful and sinful?

Unless you have a clear picture of yourself in your new identity in Christ, you are an easy mark for the enemy to trip with his lies, slander, and roadblocks. My friend, author and physician Saundra Dalton-Smith, in a recent issue of *Leading Hearts* magazine, explained, "Clarify your vision of who you are. Every patient who enters my medical practice must show proof of identification. Identity is a part of health and wellness. Disastrous things can happen when there is confusion about who you are. You wouldn't want to be given a prescription for something you don't need."[1]

So true! Ask any patient who, through mistaken identity, got the wrong prescription or had the wrong operation. Yikes! Or ask the man who stood up from his seat on the bus to allow an elderly lady to have it.

"Come on!" the little old lady said, looking up. "You can sit in my lap."

The man reddened. "Are you talking to me?"

The lady scowled. "Not unless you're my five-year-old grandson," she said as she opened her arms to the child.

It's important not only that you know who you are but also that you know your place. After all, you are no longer required to sit in the seat the evil one has saved for you. You've been given a promotion to be seated in heavenly places, as the apostle Paul explained in Ephesians 2:4–6: "But because of his great love for us, God, who is rich in mercy, made us alive with Christ even when we were dead in transgressions—it is by grace you have been saved. And God raised us up with Christ and seated us with him in the heavenly realms in Christ Jesus."

This very picture is what makes the evil one tremble. What is he so afraid of? He's afraid you are going to understand who you really are.

I'd like to take you out of your comfort zone. First, imagine Jesus in heaven seated on his throne. Can you picture it? Now, can you picture that you are seated beside him? No, not on his throne but next to him. He's so close you could lean over and whisper, "Yo, Jesus, can I ask you something?"

Our relationship with Christ is as intimate as all that? It is. What I'm trying to say is that we are in God's throne room even though our feet are still on Earth. What exactly is the throne room? David Wilkerson explained it like this: "This throne room is the seat of all power and dominion. It's the place where God rules over all principalities and powers, and reigns over the affairs of men. Here in the throne room, he monitors every move of Satan and examines every thought of man."[2]

On a sticky note, using stick figures, I drew a picture of myself being seated with Christ. I put this note on my bathroom mirror so that every time I look at myself I see who I really am. My picture shows Jesus on his throne. And there I am, stick-figure Linda, sitting right next to him with a big smile on my face. Beneath us is an arrow pointing downward to a very unhappy face. This is the face of stick-figure Satan. He's not too happy that I am seated over him, with Christ. Whoa. This is heavy. I mean, I'm seated with Christ in heavenly places, and the enemy is under my feet.

This picture is not just for me; this picture also applies to you. *You* are seated with Christ in heavenly places, and the enemy is under *your* feet. When this picture trickles down into your understanding of your identity, it's a game changer. Then when you couple who you are *with* Christ with who you are *in* Christ, it will make your head spin.

Our Quest

The apostle Paul tells us, "Put on your new nature, created to be like God—truly righteous and holy" (Eph. 4:24 NLT). To become clothed in God's holiness and righteousness so as to accomplish our purposes, we need to be clear on who God is and who we are in him. Otherwise, we will find ourselves naked and ashamed, an easy target for the schemes and lies of Satan.

So who is God? I think the best answer is that he is bigger than we could possibly imagine, more mysterious than we can fathom, and more loving than we can measure. He's the Creator, our Redeemer, and though he's bigger than the whole world, he can fit his very Spirit into our hearts.

Who are we in God? Through Christ, we

- are alive in him (Eph. 2:5)
- have his mind (1 Cor. 2:16)
- are free from the law of sin and death (Rom. 8:2)
- are holy (1 Pet. 1:16)
- are made right with him (Rom. 5:17)
- have our needs supplied by him (Phil. 4:19)
- have authority and power over the enemy (Luke 10:17–19)
- are physical temples of the Holy Spirit (1 Cor. 6:19)
- are created to do good works (Eph. 2:10)
- are more than conquerors (Rom. 8:37)

If we could get this understanding deep into our spirits, it would change everything. In Mezana's story, we see what happens to one who doesn't yet understand who she really is.

Mezana's Quest

The day Mezana followed Asriel out of her prison, it was as if she'd become a new person. The horrors of her past were behind her as she settled into a beautiful new town with a lovely cottage all to herself. At last she was free of the grime, the rags, and the rotting food.

But as clean as she looked on the outside, she still felt the guilt of her former life on the inside. Sometimes, when she was in the market, she could see the other women whisper when she passed. She understood their mistrust. If they knew all the things she'd done to survive, they'd probably banish her from the town altogether. In fact, whenever she looked in the mirror, she still saw the mess of a girl she used to be. Her own wickedness reflected back at her with a sneer.

One day when Mezana was out in the market, she heard a familiar voice whisper, "Come with me, Mezana."

Seeing no one, she hesitated, but the whisper persisted. Step-by-step she followed the sound of her name until her hair began to prickle at the nape of her neck. She suddenly saw the leers of a nearby cluster of men. She turned to flee, and as she did, the evil one blocked her escape.

He grabbed her shoulders. "Thank you for joining me at my brothel," he told her, "for this is where you truly belong."

Mezana stepped back. "I, I've been bought by another."

The evil one laughed softly. "But we both know who you really are, an immoral, disgusting creature, perfect for the abuses I have planned for you."

Mezana suddenly felt weak. What the evil one was saying about her was true. She didn't deserve the care or protection Asriel had provided her.

The evil one held out his hand. "Come. You know this is your destiny."

Somehow, Mezana felt both sick and mesmerized. Without realizing it, she took a step toward the evil one.

"Mezana!"

When she heard her name, she turned to see Asriel. "Come with me, Mezana. The evil one is no longer your master. Do not let him deceive you with his lies."

Mezana stood frozen between the two men.

"You know what you really are," the evil one said. "Come back to me."

"He's lying to you, Mezana. You are free. You are pure. You are beautiful."

Mezana turned to Asriel. "How can you say this?"

"I say this because it is true. It is true because you are mine and because you are under my protection."

Mezana fell into Asriel's arms, sobbing. When she turned to look back at the evil one, he was gone.

Asriel was right. The words the evil one had spoken to her were nothing more than lies. She was free. She was loved. And in the eyes of Asriel, she was beautiful. She never had to go back to being the person she'd been before Asriel set her free. She'd made a mistake when she'd followed the evil one's voice, but it was a mistake Asriel forgave. Perhaps she didn't deserve her benefactor, but he loved her anyway. And that was more than she could ask for. It was more than she deserved.

The Allegory Explained

Mezana did not expect to see her enemy in her new life, yet there he was, calling to her to follow him as he tried to steal her newfound identity. His lies almost worked, as she seemed, at least temporarily, to forget that she'd been bought at a great price and was no longer a slave to sin.

Mezana's experience once again reflects our own journey. We forget too. We make mistakes too. But we serve a God who remains willing to forgive us when we turn back to him. And we mustn't forget what the apostle John said in 1 John 4:4: "But you belong to God, my dear children. You have already won a victory over those people, because the Spirit who lives in you is greater than the spirit who lives in the world" (NLT).

But how do we keep our eyes focused on our new identity? We do it by keeping our eyes on Jesus. As we look to him, we are transformed into his image.

There was an old stone well behind the farmhouse on my grandfather's east Texas farm. On really hot days my brother and I would slide off the metal lid and lean our faces into the cool darkness, watching the water catch the light. We could feel the water's refreshing breath even on the hottest of days. My mother wouldn't let us kids drink from that old well, but back in the day it supplied refreshing, cool water to quench the thirst of all who drank. It's the same with us. We have a hidden oasis in Christ. We can take a refreshing drink by keeping our thoughts on him, by reading his Word, by talking to him, and by remembering that his own Holy Spirit is inside of us.

But beyond knowing who God is and better understanding our identity in Christ, we need to quit pretending that the battle raging around us is someone else's fight. It is our battle, and through Christ, it's a battle we can win. We can take the enemy's territory as we fight the good fight over our lives, purposes, homes, churches, and communities.

Just ask Elijah. Elijah was a man who knew his true identity (a servant of the Most High God) as well as God's identity (the

Lord of the universe). This understanding armed him with the gumption to challenge Queen Jezebel's 450 priests of Baal.

Four hundred and fifty against one? Was that fair?

Not really, for Elijah represented the one true God. And Jezebel's priests? They represented only a block of wood.

Team Baal was instructed to build an altar and to call on their god to ignite their offering with a blast of fire. But though the priests cried, danced, and cut themselves all day long, nothing happened except an occasional taunt from Elijah: "Shout louder! . . . I'm sure Baal is a god! Perhaps he has too much to think about. Or maybe he has gone to the toilet. Or perhaps he's away on a trip. Maybe he's sleeping. You might have to wake him up" (1 Kings 18:27 NIrV).

When it was Elijah's turn, he took the challenge a step further. He dug a trench around his own altar to Jehovah, then instructed that four jars of water be filled and poured over the altar three times until water soaked the offering and the wood and overflowed the trench.

Then Elijah prayed:

> Lord, you are the God of Abraham, Isaac and Israel. Today let everyone know that you are God in Israel. Let them know I'm your servant. Let them know I've done all these things because you commanded me to. Answer me. Lord, answer me. Then these people will know that you are the one and only God. They'll know that you are turning their hearts back to you again. (1 Kings 18:36–37 NIrV)

Kaboom! The fire of the Lord came down and licked up the sacrifice, the twelve stones of the altar, the soil, and even the water in the ditches.

There was a stunned silence. Then the men of Jerusalem turned on the false prophets of Baal and killed them.

Elijah knew who God was, and he knew he belonged to God. That's why he was able to be so bold and to rescue his people. Think of the miraculous ways God could use you if you were able to hold on to who you are in Christ.

Saul's Road to Damascus

Saul was a man burning with hatred for all those who followed Christ. His hate ran so deep that he went to the high priest in Jerusalem and asked for permission to go to the synagogue in Damascus so he could arrest the believers there.

But along the way, you might say his plans got tripped up by Jesus himself. A blinding light enveloped him, and he fell to the ground as he heard the words, "Saul! Saul! Why are you persecuting me?" (Acts 9:4 NLT).

Saul must have been terrified. Here he was on a mission from God, and now he was face-to-face with an unknown being.

"Who are you, lord?" Saul asked (Acts 9:5 NLT).

How shocked Saul must have felt when the voice replied, "I am Jesus, the one you are persecuting!" (Acts 9:5 NLT).

Jesus! Saul knew Jesus. Jesus was his enemy. Jesus was dead and buried. But here he was *alive*? In an instant, Saul realized that what Jesus's disciples and followers had claimed was true. Jesus, his enemy, *was* the foretold Messiah. He had been too blind to see it!

Jesus continued, "Now get up and go into the city, and you will be told what you must do" (Acts 9:6 NLT).

The only problem was Saul had been struck blind, reflecting the blindness of his soul. He had to be led into the city of Damascus by his companions. There he waited three days until Ananias, one of the very people Saul had come to arrest, came to him and prayed for his healing. When Ananias prayed, the scales fell from Saul's eyes. He was a new man who could see who Jesus really was! The Messiah, the Son of God! Saul didn't hesitate. He was baptized into the kingdom of Jesus Christ.

Saul, who began to call himself Paul, later summed up both his and our new identity in Christ by saying, "For if a man belongs to Christ, he is a new person. The old life is gone. New life has begun. All this comes from God. He is the One Who brought us to Himself when we hated Him. He did this through Christ. Then He gave us the work of bringing others to Him" (2 Cor. 5:17–18 NLV).

The Armor

A thousand years before Paul ran into Jesus on the road to Damascus, a shepherd boy named David was sent by his father to check on his brothers who were serving in King Saul's army. Young David, who'd only just arrived in camp with a delivery of bread and cheese, was shocked to see that a lone soldier from the Philistine army had sent the Israelite army scurrying for cover. David watched as Goliath stood in the gully between the two armies and shouted up at the army of Israel:

> Why have you come out dressed for battle? Am I not the
> Philistine, and you the servants of Saul? Choose a man for

yourselves, and let him come down to me. If he is able to fight with me and kill me, then we will be your servants. But if I fight him and kill him, then you must become our servants and work for us. . . . I stand against the army of Israel this day. Give me a man, that we may fight together. (1 Sam. 17:8–10 NLV)

Young David couldn't believe his eyes. Sure, this challenger was nine feet nine inches tall and covered from head to toe with armor, but David knew this giant was no match for God. David looked at the cowering soldiers around him and asked, "Who is this pagan Philistine anyway, that he is allowed to defy the armies of the living God?" (1 Sam. 17:26 NLT).

When King Saul heard of David's question, he called the lad before him. David told the king, "Don't worry about this Philistine. . . . I'll go fight him!" (1 Sam. 17:32 NLT).

Though King Saul tried to talk David out of the fight, David exclaimed, "The Lord Who saved me from the foot of the lion and from the foot of the bear, will save me from the hand of this Philistine."

So Saul told David, "Go, and may the Lord be with you" (1 Sam. 17:37 NLV).

But there was a kink in David's battle plan. King Saul dressed David in his own armor, signifying that David was fighting in Saul's name.

David said, "'I cannot go with these, for I am not used to them.' And David took them off. He took his stick in his hand, and chose five smooth stones from the river. He put them in his shepherd's bag. His sling was in his hand, and he went to the Philistine" (1 Sam. 17:39–40 NLV).

David rushed toward the laughing Goliath, shouting:

> You come to me with a sword and spears. But I come to you in the name of the Lord of All, the God of the armies of Israel, Whom you have stood against. This day the Lord will give you into my hands. I will knock you down and cut off your head. This day I will give the dead bodies of the army of the Philistines to the birds of the sky and the wild animals of the earth. Then all the earth may know that there is a God in Israel. All these people gathered here may know that the Lord does not save with sword and spear. For the battle is the Lord's and He will give you into our hands. (1 Sam. 17:45–47 NLV)

David slung the stone and whap! It hit the giant right between the eyes. With a great crash, Goliath fell to the earth, and David grabbed the giant's own sword and sliced off his head.

I so love what David was wearing! David won the victory clothed in the name of the Lord! Suiting up in the name of the Lord is exactly what we must do as well. This is what wearing the armor of God is all about.

Suiting Up

The apostle Paul described the armor that is available to us in Ephesians 6:10–17:

> A final word: Be strong in the Lord and in his mighty power. Put on all of God's armor so that you will be able to stand firm against all strategies of the devil. For we are not fighting against flesh-and-blood enemies, but against evil rulers and authorities of the unseen world, against mighty powers

in this dark world, and against evil spirits in the heavenly places.

Therefore, put on every piece of God's armor so you will be able to resist the enemy in the time of evil. Then after the battle you will still be standing firm. Stand your ground, putting on the belt of truth and the body armor of God's righteousness. For shoes, put on the peace that comes from the Good News so that you will be fully prepared. In addition to all of these, hold up the shield of faith to stop the fiery arrows of the devil. Put on salvation as your helmet, and take the sword of the Spirit, which is the word of God. (NLT)

There is no need to fear, especially when we understand the armor and the weapons. The armor and the weapons were given to us by God himself not only to protect us but also to help us win the victory against the enemy. Lysa TerKeurst says, "It would be foolish to go out into public without your physical clothing, but even more foolish to leave your spiritual armor behind. The battles are real—we must be prepared."[3]

Dear Lord,
Please teach me how to wear your armor so that I may be clothed in you. Show me your secrets to defeat the enemy at every turn. In Jesus's name, amen.

ARMORED RESPONSE

Just like David, you can declare that you wear the name of the Lord and go against any giants who harass you.

Giant-Fighting Scripture

"But I come to you in the name of the Lord of All, the God of the armies of Israel, Whom you have stood against. This day the Lord will give you into my hands" (1 Sam. 17:45 NLV).

Declaration to Defeat Giants

I declare that I come against problems, hindrances, and harassments from the enemy in the name of the Lord Jesus, the Lord of all, whom the enemy stands against. This day the Lord is giving me victory over my problems, hindrances, and harassments. The giants are defeated in the name of Jesus. I know whose I am. I belong to Jesus, and I know that he is in me and has transformed me. I call on all of his power.

Prayer for Victory over Giants

Dear Lord,

Forgive me for cowering in fear while the giants in my life taunt me. I thank you that I can put on your name and face these giants. I not only put on your name but also call on your name to cancel the assignments of these giants. Nail these assignments to the cross, erasing them from my life. I ask you, Lord, to give me victory through the power of the name and the blood of Jesus and through the empowerment of God's Holy Spirit. Amen.

3

Wearing the Truth of Christ

Stand your ground, putting on the belt of truth.

Ephesians 6:14 NLT

Molly was a publicist who really seemed interested in helping me get the word out about my books. One day I got a call from Carly, one of my prayer partners who also used Molly's services. Carly said, "Molly told me she printed twenty thousand copies of my new book."

"That's a lot of books," I said.

"The problem is she printed my book six months ago and I have yet to see a single copy."

"That's odd. What does Molly say about that?"

"She's full of excuses," Carly explained. "The latest is she's out of copies. She said she had to send the last book to fulfill a huge order with a nationwide bookstore chain. She says she needs more money so she can print more books."

"Didn't you get a final proof of the book before it went to press?"

"No."

"Then who edited it?"

"Molly did."

"And you didn't proof her edits?"

"She didn't give me the chance."

"Did she at least send you payment for the books sold or an invoice for the books printed?"

"Nothing. I've seen nothing even though I've sent her checks for thousands of dollars."

"Hmmm. How about the two of us pray over this," I suggested. So we did. We prayed, "Dear Lord, please show us your truth in this matter."

At the end of our prayer, Carly confided, "If I could just see a photo of the books in the warehouse, that would really help me believe everything's okay. I mean, I so want to believe Molly is telling me the truth."

Moments later, while Carly and I were saying our good-byes, we both received an email from Molly. The email contained a picture with the caption "Carly's books in the warehouse."

Carly lowered her voice. "Do you think it's possible Molly can hear us?"

"We're thousands of miles apart," I said. "How could she?"

"I don't know, but don't you think it's strange she sent this particular photo to both of us just now? It feels like she's trying to answer our prayers."

"Something's off," I agreed. "Perhaps you should call the bookstore chain and ask them if they carry your book." The next day the news wasn't good. The chain had never heard of Carly or her book. They had certainly never ordered it.

I too had a few questions about several PR projects that had no record of completion. Then through a little internet sleuthing, I discovered Molly was operating under a pseudonym and was actually a known con artist.

That's when I remembered an incident. A few months back Molly had emailed me what was supposed to be a photo. However, when I tried to open the file, no photo appeared. When I called her about it, she said, "Oops, I sent you the wrong file. Let me send the photo again." The next download opened to an unremarkable photo of an ordinary daisy, a strange picture to send me I'd thought at the time. But now, as I read an article about other cons Molly had orchestrated, the lightbulb switched on as I thought about that daisy photo. I realized the first file Molly had sent me was spyware, which I'd activated when I downloaded it. The spyware had allowed Molly to take control of my computer so she could both watch and listen to me and read whatever I typed.

My computer guy soon confirmed my suspicions before he wiped her spyware off my machine.

As it turned out, Molly had scammed dozens of my author friends to a tune of hundreds of thousands of dollars! Carly and I believe it was our prayer seeking God's truth that cracked open the case and stopped the theft of our hopes and dreams and those of our author friends.[1]

Molly, a very talented woman, now uses her spyware to run an online psychic scam. But Molly is actually the victim of the biggest con of all. She traded God's true purpose for her for money. What she did is in fact a common mistake: letting the lies of the enemy keep us from our true callings.

The way to keep from being the victim of such a con is to seek God's truth in the matter of our purposes.

In fact, truth is the mark of a believer. Jesus said, "You are truly my disciples if you remain faithful to my teachings. And you will know the truth, and the truth will set you free" (John 8:31–32 NLT).

Truth is what we all need, and we need it in every area of our lives because the enemy is a con man. Jesus described him this way: "He was a murderer from the beginning. He has always hated the truth, because there is no truth in him. When he lies, it is consistent with his character; for he is a liar and the father of lies" (John 8:44 NLT).

Our Quest

The first piece of armor Paul tells us to put on is truth: "Stand your ground, putting on the belt of truth" (Eph. 6:14 NLT). This all-important piece of gear is one of our best weapons against Satan and includes the truth of who Jesus Christ is, the truth of what Jesus did for us, the truth of who we are in Christ, the truth that Jesus loves us, and the truth that we each have been called to a purpose.

These are the truths that will lead us to transformation and will equip us for our daily battles. This is why we need to stay in the truth of God's Word, for God's Word is the perfect antidote to the enemy's lies. Yes, Satan is still a liar, even though Jesus defeated him on the cross.

Rick Stedman said, "Fortunately, into our world of deep and deceptive darkness, Jesus came to shine the light. The bad news is that Satan lies 100 percent of the time; the good news is that Jesus is 100 percent truthful. Jesus said, 'I am the way, the truth, and the life' (John 14:6). When we put on the belt of truth, his light, love, and truthfulness shine in us."[2]

Let's look at our continuing story of Mezana and Asriel to see how putting on the truth of Christ can make all the difference.

Mezana's Quest

Mezana stared at her reflection in the mirror and saw the truth: she was a broken and unlovable girl. She touched the scar on her cheek made when her former master, the evil one, had lashed her with his whip. "No one will ever love you now," he'd sneered as blood ran down her face. "You are scarred forever by my brand."

Mezana's hand trembled as she pulled her hair back from her scar and stared at the jagged, red stripe. She sighed as she thought of what Asriel would say at the sight of the scar. To even imagine that he could love her was no longer possible. It was only a matter of time until he saw her the way she saw herself, before he sent her back into the nightmare that had defined her life.

Mezana rose and pulled her shawl around her shoulders and hurried outside into the cool of the evening. The sun had just dipped beyond the horizon. She'd not seen Asriel all day. In fact, she hadn't seen him since he'd rescued her at the brothel. Maybe he, like all of her former lovers, had already abandoned her.

The chill Mezana felt in her soul prickled her skin as she wandered the dark path to the sea, blinded by both the darkness and her tears. She approached the sound of the pounding surf and soon felt the waves lap at her feet. She heard the night breeze whisper to her, "Keep walking until the water surrounds you, until the waves wash over your head. Let the darkness welcome you as you escape this world with death."

Mezana hesitated at the command. Should she? She dropped her shawl on the beach and slipped out of her sandals before stepping into the water.

"Keep walking, Mezana. No one can love you, not even Asriel."

Mezana pushed her body deeper toward the whispers.

"This is your only escape."

The water was to her chest now, and she knew it would take her into its blackness.

A voice called her name. "Mezana!" She turned to see Asriel standing on the shore.

A wave hit her from behind, knocking her beneath the water. The roar of the water drowned out Asriel's voice, and all she could hear was the dark whisper, "Give in to the darkness. Surrender to me."

She tumbled beneath the surface, pinned to the rough sand under the waves. Her lungs burned as she breathed a mouthful of brine. Suddenly, strong hands reached for her as all faded to black. The next thing she knew she was on the shore wrapped in a blanket and sitting by a warm fire. Asriel pulled a piece of seaweed from her matted hair. She blushed knowing he'd seen her scarred cheek in the firelight. She turned her face away as she managed to mumble, "I am too ugly."

"That's not how I see you."

Asriel cupped her face in his hands. "Mezana, you are so precious."

Mezana stared into his loving eyes and asked, "Do you not see my scar?"

Asriel touched her cheek. "What scar?"

Mezana brushed her finger against her suddenly smooth cheek, and she blinked. What had just happened?

"In my love, you are transformed."

"For what purpose?"

"To be loved, to love—but all will be revealed. For now you must trust me. You must stay away from the whispers of darkness and walk in the light of my truth."

With that, Asriel handed her a gift wrapped in bright paper. As Mezana pulled away the wrappings, she began to uncoil a leather belt covered with shimmering disks of gold.

"It's beautiful," Mezana managed to whisper.

"When you wear it, it will help you discern what is true."

"Then I will wear it always," Mezana said as she buckled the belt around her.

Asriel smiled. "This is good news, for there will come a day when this belt of truth will save your life."

The Allegory Explained

On the ThinkingAboutSuicide.com website that I manage, I often hear suicidal people lament, "God doesn't love me. I might as well be dead." This idea of God failing to love us is nothing but a lie of the enemy. Unfortunately, it is one of many lies whispered by the evil one.

The truth is God's love for us is real and does transform us. Despite our scars, God sees us as precious. And no matter how we may *feel*, the truth is we have a purpose: to love and to be loved. It is not God's will that we be deceived. However, the enemy of our souls will deceive us whenever he can with lies, half-truths, and feelings we shouldn't trust. John the evangelist wrote in 1 John 4:1–3:

> Dear friends, do not believe every spirit, but test the spirits to see whether they are from God, because many false prophets have gone out into the world. This is how you can recognize the Spirit of God: Every spirit that acknowledges that Jesus Christ has come in the flesh is from God, but every spirit that does not acknowledge Jesus is not from God. This is the spirit of the antichrist, which you have heard is coming and even now is already in the world.

Jesus told us in John 10:10, "The thief comes only to steal and kill and destroy." What does our enemy want to steal? He wants to steal our very souls. But once our souls belong to Jesus, he has his eye on other prizes, including our purpose, mission, peace, sound mind, joy, and victory in Christ. Of course, he also wants to blind us to truth. The battle is not over, and we must be on guard, as Paul explains in 2 Corinthians 11:3–4:

> But I fear that somehow your pure and undivided devotion to Christ will be corrupted, just as Eve was deceived by the cunning ways of the serpent. You happily put up with whatever anyone tells you, even if they preach a different Jesus than the one we preach, or a different kind of Spirit than the one you received, or a different kind of gospel than the one you believed.

Please do not assume that every good-sounding teaching is from God. Eve saw that the tree of life was "good," but her desire for this "good" was not of God. She disobeyed God when she bit into the forbidden fruit, causing her eyes to be opened to the bitterness of sin and death. We must not stray from God's Word based on what we feel is good. We must instead be careful to follow God's truth in all things. Just as Carly and I prayed for truth over a confusing situation with Molly, we must all pray for God's truth to reveal itself over all that is counterfeit. Then when God reveals any hidden deceptions, we must seek him for the solutions to right any wrongs the deceptions caused.

The Apostle Paul's Story Continues

Saul, whom we will now refer to as the apostle Paul, met truth when he met Jesus on the road to Damascus, an encounter that changed his life. So instead of pursuing and throwing Christians into prison, Paul pursued Christ and followed his will. He traveled the roads and seas of the Middle East, preaching, healing the sick, and casting out demons in the name of Jesus.

Paul was a sensation in the ancient city of Ephesus, mainly because he powerfully wielded the name of Jesus to set people free from demonic oppressions. The believers of Ephesus were grateful. With all the worship of false gods happening in town, they certainly understood the heartache of demonic oppression.

Today many Christians are blind to the truth about the dangers of the darkness and go about entertaining the demonic. They indulge in dark movies, pornography, affairs, tarot cards, fortune-tellers, séances, drug abuse, and the like, all door openers to the whispers, lies, and oppression of Satan. Many believers today do not seem to realize the danger of opening these doors of darkness.

The believers of ancient Ephesus knew better. They saw the connection between heartaches and spiritual evil because it was constantly illustrated through the goings-on at their city's temple, which was dedicated to the false goddess Artemus, also known as Dianna. So when Paul showed up in town to build a church for Jesus Christ, a church that could cast out demons and heal the sick, many of the people of Ephesus were swayed to follow Christ to freedom.

Staying in the truth was of utmost importance to Paul, who once wrote to his coworker for Christ, young Timothy, "Do your best to present yourself to God as one approved, a worker who does not need to be ashamed and who correctly handles the word of truth" (2 Tim. 2:15).

We too should heed Paul's advice and learn, as Paul taught, not only to handle the Word of Truth correctly but also to wear it around our waist like a belt.

The Armor

As we noted in Ephesians 6:10–18, the first piece of armor Paul recommends is truth: "Stand therefore, having girded your waist with truth" (v. 14 NKJV).

This verse seems to imply that the armor of God comes with a girdle. But this girdle is not about binding the body into a slimming silhouette; it instead describes a belt that we can use to hitch our robes high so we do not become entangled when we need to be fast on our feet. A Roman soldier's girdle also had a wide leather fringe covered with bits of metal to protect his groin, plus it was the perfect place to tether a knife or sword.

The purpose of our belt of truth is to give us clarity about who we are in Christ and our callings and purposes. God's truth (his Word) will not only protect our vulnerabilities but will also keep us from being entangled in the enemy's deception as we put on the person of truth (Jesus Christ) through his Holy Spirit (the Spirit of truth).

Mark Bubeck wrote this about the belt of truth:

> Satan hates to face the believer who has the belt of truth buckled around his waist. Have you ever told a lie convincingly then suddenly the truth came out? There you were, caught in your lie, absolutely devastated. The belt of truth affects Satan and his kingdom in the same way. It devastates and totally defeats him. It exposes his deceiving lying ways for what they are and breaks his power against you.[3]

Suiting Up

Our fight against the dark world is ongoing, so we must remain battle ready, careful that we are never caught without the truth of Christ tied around us. The enemy of our souls was present at the dawn of time, and he's had centuries to watch us, observe us, and study our human weaknesses. He knows how to tempt us at our most vulnerable moments. It's not okay to take off our armor while we follow the nudges of the enemy into sin, even if only for a moment. It's moments like those when the enemy of our souls springs his traps to capture us in compromising positions.

The belt of truth—combined with prayer—can break people out of the strong delusion that right is wrong and wrong is right. The belt of truth can bar deception while it sets us free from the strategies of the enemy.

My friend Ann and I tied on the belt of truth in prayer one Sunday afternoon when she called me in desperation. Her son's best friend, Jack, had jumped from a cliff above a raging river. He had gone under the rapids and disappeared. The water was so dangerous that the rescue workers had refused to retrieve his body. That's when her son Dale decided he would retrieve Jack's body by tying one end of a rope around his waist and the other end around a tree before jumping in. On the way to the river Dale had stopped by his mother's house to tell her good-bye.

Ann called to tell me, "I tried to stop him and I couldn't. If he jumps into the river, the current will pin him down too, regardless of how strong he thinks he is. You have to pray!"

"No, *you* have to pray," I told her. "You have to pray in the full armor of God, in the knowing of who you are in Jesus, for the armor *is* Jesus."

Ann led us in a prayer as she prayed the armor on herself and on her son, especially the belt of truth. An hour later she called me back.

"Ann, what happened?"

"Dale got to the river and decided not to jump. Do you know what a miracle that is?"

"I do."

The belt of truth made the difference. As Dale was preparing to jump, Jack's mother told him the truth. "I believe Jack committed suicide. Please do not add to the body count." It was this truth that changed Dale's mind and kept him from doing something that would have certainly taken his life and resulted in *two* funerals.[4]

You might be wondering why I told Ann that the armor *is* Jesus. Compare each piece of the armor with the truth of who Jesus is.

- Belt of truth: Jesus is the truth. "Jesus said to him, 'I am the way, the truth, and the life. No one comes to the Father except through Me'" (John 14:6 NKJV).
- Breastplate of righteousness: Jesus is righteousness. "My dear children, I write this to you so that you will not sin. But if anybody does sin, we have an advocate with the Father—Jesus Christ, the Righteous One" (1 John 2:1).
- Sandals of peace: Jesus is the Prince of Peace. "And he will be called: Wonderful Counselor, Mighty God, Everlasting Father, Prince of Peace" (Isa. 9:6 NLT).
- Shield of faith: Jesus is the source of our faith. "Let us run with endurance the race that is set before us, looking unto Jesus, the author and finisher of our faith" (Heb. 12:1–2 NKJV).
- Helmet of salvation: Jesus is our salvation. "No one else can save us. Indeed, we can be saved only by the power of the one named Jesus and not by any other person" (Acts 4:12 GW).
- Sword of the Spirit (God's Word): Jesus is the Word. "The Word (Christ) was in the beginning. The Word was with God. The Word was God. He

was with God in the beginning. He made all things.
Nothing was made without Him making it. Life
began by Him. His Life was the Light for men.
The Light shines in the darkness. The darkness has
never been able to put out the Light" (John 1:1–5
NLV).

So when we put on the armor of Christ, we are putting on
Jesus himself. In fact, Romans 13:14 says, "But be clothed
with the Lord Jesus Christ" (JUB). Knowing that when we
put on the armor we are putting on Christ is a great perspective changer, for now we know:

- We are in Christ (2 Cor. 5:17).
- Christ is in us (Col. 1:27).
- We are hidden or clothed in Christ (Rom. 13:14;
  Col. 3:3).

Dear Lord,

*I buckle your truth around my waist and agree that I
am in you. I also agree that you are in me and that I am
completely hidden or clothed in you. You are my truth, you
are my righteousness, you are my peace, you are the author
and finisher of my faith, you are my salvation, and both
your Word and your Spirit are alive in me.*

*Keep me in your truth. Open my eyes to any deception
or lie of the enemy. Give me your solutions to all the lies
I've believed as you reveal your truth. I pray this with and
in and through and in agreement with you and in your
name. Amen.*

ARMORED RESPONSE

The best way to defeat the lies of the enemy is to embrace truth.

Lie-Fighting Scripture

"When the Spirit of Truth comes, he will guide you into the full truth. He won't speak on his own. He will speak what he hears and will tell you about things to come" (John 16:13 GW).

Declaration to Defeat Lies

I declare that the Spirit of truth has come in the form of the Holy Spirit. I invite him to have an even greater place in my life. I declare that the Holy Spirit guides me to full truth as he tells me what the Father wants me to know, the things I need to know, now and in the future.

Prayer for Victory over Lies

Dear Lord,

Forgive me for allowing any unbelief into my heart, for I choose to believe in you. Please help me overcome any temptation to doubt as you help me and teach me by your Holy Spirit residing in me. Teach me your deeper truths—how to discern your truth and how to keep my trust in you. Show me what the enemy wants to hide from me, and give me your solutions to overcome his lies. In Jesus's name, amen.

4

Wearing the
Righteousness of Christ

Stand your ground, putting on the . . . body armor of God's
righteousness.

Ephesians 6:14 NLT

It was a hot July night, so hot that the police officer took off
his bulletproof vest so he could cool down. No one was on
the streets at 4:30 a.m. anyway. But as he patrolled a section
of the city, he noticed some men walking by. That's when the
officer felt the hair on the back of his neck rise and heard a
voice tell him to grab his vest and put it on, a voice he believes
was the voice of God.

It's a good thing he heeded that voice, because shortly
thereafter a car pulled up behind him and a man began shoot-
ing. Though the officer was hit, he survived the bullet with
only a bruise. The vest had kept the bullet from penetrating
his heart and saved his life.[1]

This is exactly what the "body armor" or, as other translations call it, "breastplate of righteousness," as described by Paul in Ephesians 6:14, is meant to do. It is meant to protect us.

Our Quest

Paul implores us to "stand your ground, putting on the . . . body armor of God's righteousness" (Eph. 6:14 NLT).

Just knowing about the armor won't protect us. We must put the armor on in order for it to protect our hearts. This piece of armor works in two ways. First, it allows us to wear Christ's righteousness over our unrighteousness. His righteousness makes us holy enough to walk with God and also protects us like a bulletproof vest by deflecting the accusations the enemy would use to wound, cripple, and discredit us and to stop us from accomplishing our God-given purposes. Second, covering ourselves with Christ's righteousness keeps our hearts from betraying us and helps us make the right decisions. Rick Stedman tells a story about a man who pulled off his watch and flipped it over so Rick could read the inscription: "To my husband on our wedding day. Follow your heart." The man explained that by following these words he had made poor decisions. The man said, "When I was tempted, I followed my heart and ended up doing things that led to the ruin of our marriage."[2]

I'm not blaming the wife for putting what she thought was a beautiful inscription on her husband's wedding gift. After all, her idea was that she would be the one her husband's heart would follow. But what she didn't realize is that, left unchecked, a human heart makes a poor moral compass. That's why we need to wear the breastplate of righteousness. As Paul explained to the Ephesians, "You used to live in sin, just like the rest of the world, obeying the devil—the commander of the powers in the unseen world. He is the spirit at work in the hearts of those who refuse to obey God" (Eph. 2:2 NLT). Allowing the evil one's spirit to direct our lives is horrifyingly unimaginable and completely avoidable.

Mezana's Quest

Mezana awoke in her bed wondering if last night had been a bad dream. Had she really almost given in to the taunts of the darkness? She wouldn't have believed it if it hadn't been for her damp robes drying on a nearby chair.

Now in the morning's light, she brushed her matted hair and contemplated how to avoid the shadows. She would have avoided the entire day, hiding behind her bolted door, if her cupboard hadn't been bare. But her hunger forced her to put herself together as best she could. She decided her clothes were dry enough to wear, but as she searched for her sandals and shawl, she remembered how she'd dropped them on the beach. Her heart sank knowing they were lost, carried away by the waves. Her only protection from the damp chill was her old tattered shawl, the one she had worn as a slave girl.

Barefoot, Mezana hurried to the market, hoping no one would notice that her sandals and beautiful shawl were missing. With a pounding headache, she wasn't up to the questions of the curious vendors. She was relieved that her purchases of bread and a few vegetables seemed to go unnoticed.

At least, that's what she thought, until she slipped into the door of her abode.

When she tried to shut the door behind her, it flung open as a dirty man pushed his way inside.

"I'm glad I found you, Mezana."

She stepped back. "Beliah, what are you doing here?"

Beliah grabbed her arm and pulled her to him. "I saw you in the marketplace, and I knew I could come here and take whatever I needed." He pulled the loaf of bread from her hand and bit into it.

Mezana's voice shook. "This is not your house."

"I saw you're still wearing your shawl, the one given to you by our master. You still belong to him, and that gives me the right to do with you as I wish."

Mezana pulled her arm free. "You're wrong. I no longer belong to the evil one."

"And this house," Beliah said, "will be my house whenever I'm in town, and you, you will be mine."

"Get out!" Mezana said. "I now belong to another."

"Then tell me his price. I will gladly pay it whenever I visit."

"I am not for sale."

"You? Not for sale?" Beliah laughed. "What kind of fool do you think I am? I know what you are."

Mezana stepped back. "If my master comes and finds you here, surely he will kill you."

Beliah spit a chunk of Mezana's bread onto the floor and stepped toward her.

"I do not see your master." He pointed at her shawl. "All I see is evidence that you are mine for the taking."

A soft knock sounded at the door, and Mezana brushed past Beliah as she rushed to answer. Before her stood a child holding her missing shawl. The girl said, "Asriel said you left this at the shore and asked me to return it."

Mezana smiled. "Thank you, my little friend," she said as she dropped her tattered shawl onto the stoop before draping the glowing, white shawl around her shoulders. The child hurried away as Mezana turned back to Beliah. "I was telling you the truth. See, I have on the shawl of my master, Asriel. I am under his protection." She pointed to the open door. "You must leave."

Beliah's eyes narrowed. "Asriel? What would a man like that want with the likes of you?"

"In the name of Asriel, I command you to go," Mezana said as sunlight streamed across the doorjamb.

"I will get to the bottom of this," Beliah growled as he passed her. He paused on her stoop and turned. "I'll be back. You can be assured of that."

Trembling, Mezana shut and bolted the door behind him and sank to the floor. The shawl of Asriel had saved her, a shawl she always needed to remember to wear so she could prove she was under her new master's protection. It was the only way she could stand up to her enemy's accusations.

The Allegory Explained

Just as the shawl of Asriel protected Mezana from Beliah, the righteousness of Christ is our protection against our accuser, Satan. Christ's righteousness springs our release from the enemy's camp into the kingdom of God. Neil Anderson says, "The breastplate of righteousness is the Lord's righteousness bestowed upon us. This righteousness is imputed at salvation.

Imputed righteousness means that something that belongs to one person is put on the account of another person."[3]

The righteousness of Jesus is ours, and as long as we wear it, it proves God's ownership over our lives. As the story of Mezana demonstrates, the enemy will still accuse us. But we do not have to believe or give in to his accusations because we have been bought by the blood of Jesus. The evil one is no longer our master. We have the right to tell him and his accusations to leave us in the power and authority of the name of Jesus, our Savior, our master, our Lord!

The Apostle Paul and the Viper

After Paul became a follower of Jesus, he set out on five missionary journeys, always teaching about Jesus in the local Jewish synagogues as he built the church of Jesus Christ.

But on many occasions, Paul's words about Jesus incited the Jewish leaders to arrest him. Finally, while Paul was on a visit to Jerusalem, the Jewish leaders beat him and dragged him before the Roman rulers of their land, King Agrippa and the governor, Festus. Upon examination of Paul, Agrippa and Festus found that Paul had broken none of the laws of Rome, so when Paul asked for an appeal before Caesar, Agrippa and Festus were happy to be rid of their problem. The rulers had Paul sent to Rome by ship.

But sailing the sea was not without peril, and Paul soon found himself in a terrible storm and shipwrecked on the island of Malta, a large island off the toe of Italy. The people who lived on Malta saw the wreck and came out into the storm to help the survivors with food and provisions. While Paul was placing brushwood on the fire, a viper crawled out of it and bit him, latching itself to his hand.

Paul wasn't the first biblical character to tangle with a snake. That honor belonged to Eve in the Garden of Eden. In her case, she was bitten by lies and was poisoned when she bit into sin. This bite caused an unbridgeable gap between all of humankind and God.

The children of Israel tangled with snakes as they followed Moses in the desert. The people complained against both Moses and God, and God was so angry that he sent fiery serpents to bite the people so they would die a slow and painful death. But the people repented from their sin of complaining, and God instructed Moses to create a bronze snake on a pole. Everyone who looked at the snake lived (Num. 21:8–9). In this account, which foreshadowed Christ's work on the cross, those who were poisoned were given an antidote of salvation. They were able to look with faith at a serpent (who represented Jesus becoming our sin) hanging on a pole (representing the cross).

This brings us to Paul and the snake of Malta. I think what happened next is a revelation of God's truth, meaning God used a real-life event to symbolize our own story of faith. In this case, Paul was able to shake off the viper with no ill effect. In the same way, we have been bitten by sin but can shake off the consequence of sin (eternal death) through Christ.

If we are free from the consequence of eternal death, why do we still need to wear the breastplate of righteousness? Because the breastplate of righteousness covers our old nature and shows the enemy he has no claim to us.

The enemy: Ha! I've got you now!

Us: Not so fast! You're looking at the *old* me. My sin is covered by the righteousness of Christ. Because I belong to Christ, your legal claim to me is void.

What great news! It's like Paul told the believers at Colossae:

> You were once dead because of your failures and your uncircumcised corrupt nature. But God made you alive with Christ when he forgave all our failures. He did this by erasing the charges that were brought against us by the written laws God had established. He took the charges away by nailing them to the cross. He stripped the rulers and authorities of their power and made a public spectacle of them as he celebrated his victory in Christ. (Col. 2:13–15 GW)

The Armor

Our own righteousness is like filthy rags, and the problem with filthy rags is that they do not protect us from bullets or arrows. When we wear the breastplate of the righteousness of Jesus, we are protected from the zingers the enemy hurls our way. "You're not good enough." "You don't deserve God's love." "You should be ashamed." "God will never forgive you!" "You think God is calling you to do something for him? Doesn't he know who you really are?" These accusations and lies, designed to stop us from fulfilling our purposes, cannot hit their mark. They are deflected by the righteousness of God.

In DreamWorks's 2004 movie *Shrek 2*, Princess Fiona's parents invite Fiona and her new husband, Shrek, to dinner and discover that their daughter has not only married a green ogre but also turned into one herself. At first, Fiona's father, King Harold, does everything in his power to break the union so he can get Fiona back with her former suitor, Prince Charming. In the end, when Fiona and Shrek try to seal their happily ever after with a kiss, the evil fairy godmother, Prince Charming's mother, attempts to use her dark magic against Shrek by declaring, "But ogres weren't made to live happily ever after."

Her words transform into a solid stream of evil set to destroy Shrek. But upon seeing the powerful incantation streaming toward the green ogre, King Harold springs into action, jumping in front of the evil declaration. Just when you think the king has given his life to save Shrek, the evil words deflect off the shininess of his breastplate and return to hit the fairy godmother, who poofs out of the picture.

That's what it's like when we are wearing our King's righteousness. Because our King Jesus gave his life for us, we can exchange our own filthy rags for his righteousness. The enemy's evil words and accusations cannot penetrate this armor and will poof right out of our lives.

Suiting Up

We can keep our armor in place first by choosing to put it on and then by choosing to keep it on through the power of the Holy Spirit. We must never take it off because, just like the police officer who had his body armor in place when he unexpectedly entered a gun battle, we never know when the enemy will launch an assault against us.

When we wear the breastplate of righteousness, the fiery arrows of the enemy cannot hurt us. And the more we cover ourselves with Christ's righteousness, the more we begin to make choices that line up with God's purposes for our lives. As Paul said to the church of Philippi, "And this is my prayer: that your love may abound more and more in knowledge and depth of insight, so that you may be able to discern what is best and may be pure and blameless for the day of Christ, filled with the fruit of righteousness that comes through Jesus Christ—to the glory and praise of God" (Phil. 1:9–11).

Dear Lord,

I slip into the armor of righteousness—which is the righteousness of Christ—through the power of the Holy Spirit. I exchange my filthy rags of sin for the righteousness and protection of Jesus. Lord, protect my heart with your armor of righteousness. Silence the accusations of my enemy. Help me to be on guard against the temptations of the enemy. I pray this with and in and through and in agreement with you and in your name. Amen.

ARMORED RESPONSE

The breastplate of righteousness is God's gift to us. He accepts us because he sees the righteousness of Christ instead of our sin.

Rejection-Fighting Scripture

"For everyone has sinned; we all fall short of God's glorious standard. Yet God freely and graciously declares that we are righteous. He did this through Christ Jesus when he freed us from the penalty for our sins" (Rom. 3:23–24 NLT).

Declaration to Defeat Rejection

I declare that though I have sinned and don't deserve forgiveness, the Lord will not only forgive me, but he will also accept me through the righteousness of Jesus.

Prayer for Victory over Rejection

Dear Lord,

How can I thank you for not only forgiving me for my sins but also for seeing me through the righteousness of Jesus? My praise goes out to Jesus for dying in my place so that I can walk with you and know you. In Jesus's name, amen.

5

Walking in the Gospel of Peace

For shoes, put on the peace that comes from the Good
News so that you will be fully prepared.

Ephesians 6:15 NLT

Tonight while I was dining with my hubby in our favorite restaurant, I wasn't thinking about my feet. But that was before a bat began to dive around the heads of the diners before plunging low, scraping the floor as it swooped directly toward my bare toes. All I could think of was that there was no way my sandals would protect me from a bat bite.

I diverted the bat by swinging my very large purse over my feet. Blocked by my unexpected move, the bat soared higher before taking another couple of laps around the room, almost parting my dear husband's hair. We cheered with the diners around us when the bat flew out the back door.

Since the moment that black, leathery creature swooped at my feet, I haven't stopped thinking about the importance of wearing the right footwear. Tonight, for example, I should have worn my galoshes to the restaurant.

Speaking of wearing the wrong shoes, I actually wore unfashionable footwear to a recent wedding. While all the other women guests wore strappy little sandals with their sleeveless party garb, I showed up in leather boots, long pants, and sleeves, along with my big, floppy sun hat. As the wedding was in the middle of a Rocky Mountain National Park meadow at the height of sunburn and Rocky Mountain tick fever season, I feel I made the right choice, though I may have given the guests someone to talk about.

But the time I was truly grateful for the right footwear was when I was hiking on a trail near the mountain town of Durango, Colorado. That morning I walked into a shady area and stepped into a nest of deadly baby rattlesnakes. I felt no peace until I realized the snakes were too tiny to bite me through my thick leather hiking boots. To get to safety, all I had to do was step out of their nest.

So when the apostle Paul talks about the importance of wearing the shoes of peace, I think I understand. The right footwear can make all the difference, whether we're running a race, speaking at a black-tie event, or standing in a rattlesnake nest. But we need to find out how to wear the shoes of the gospel of peace, shoes that have a special purpose we must understand.

Our Quest

Paul explained, "For shoes, put on the peace that comes from the Good News so that you will be fully prepared" (Eph. 6:15 NLT).

The purpose of the shoes of peace is twofold. First, these shoes will equip us to walk in the peace of God. Walking in God's peace has outstanding benefits: better health, less stress, greater ability to trust God in all things, deeper faith, and a happier life. Author Max Anders agrees, believing the peace of God "is ours when we believe the promises of God and act accordingly."[1] Jesus himself said, "I am leaving you with a gift—peace of mind and heart. And the peace I give is a gift the world cannot give. So don't be troubled or afraid" (John 14:27 NLT).

What about the second purpose of the shoes of peace? Author and Bible commentator Warren Wiersbe said, "The shoes have another meaning. We must be prepared each day to share the Gospel of peace to a lost world."[2] Wiersbe's thoughts go hand in hand with a beautiful passage in Isaiah, which reads, "How beautiful on the mountains are the feet of the messenger who brings good news, the good news of peace and salvation, the news that the God of Israel reigns!" (52:7 NLT).

Wiersbe reminds us, "Satan has declared war, but you and I are ambassadors of peace (2 Cor. 5:18–21); and as such, we take the gospel of peace wherever we go."[3]

Let's see how the story of Mezana reveals this.

Mezana's Quest

Mezana looked out the window to watch the little girl who had returned Asriel's shawl to her. The girl, delighting in the beauty of the day, sat beneath a shady tree and sang a song to the passing clouds. That's when Mezana noticed him. Beliah was crouching in the shadows watching the child. Mezana shuddered, remembering when she'd first met Beliah. His had been the rough hands that had abducted her from her father's tent. He had been the first of many to steal her innocence. The fact that he was now watching this cherub of a girl sent chills down her spine.

Mezana opened her door and with some urgency cried, "Child! Come in. I have something to ask of you."

When the girl was seated at her table, munching on the sliced carrots Mezana had offered her, Mezana asked, "How is it that you know Asriel?"

The girl's brown eyes glowed. "He watches over me, over all the orphans of the city."

Mezana was shocked. "You're an orphan?"

The girl nodded. "My parents were killed in a raid by the evil one."

Mezana reached over and pushed the girl's unruly curls away from her eyes. "Do raids happen here often?"

The girl nodded. "For centuries I'm told."

"But why?"

"The tribe of the evil one has always kidnapped our people. Until Asriel came, no one could stand against him."

Mezana rose and walked to the window to see if Beliah still waited. When she didn't see him, she felt relief. She reached for her pitcher to pour the child a glass of water when the front door banged open. The pitcher slipped from Mezana's hand and shattered on the stone floor.

Mezana watched in horror as Beliah pulled the girl from the table and slung her over his shoulder. Mezana stepped forward shouting, "That child does not belong to you."

Her bare foot crunched a shard of pottery, slicing her foot open. Blood mingled with the water that ran through a sea of shards, a sea that separated Mezana from the child. If only she hadn't lost her sandals at the shore!

"You cannot stop me!" Beliah scoffed as he began backing toward the door. "I will do with this child as I did to you."

"No!" Mezana screamed.

"Your shoes!" the child cried. "Behind you!"

Mezana slipped her sandals onto her feet and, once protected, ran over the broken pottery in time to grab the child's arm just as Beliah tried to escape out the door. Mezana tugged at the child and screamed for help as Asriel suddenly appeared. When Beliah saw him, he let the child slip from his grasp and into Mezana's waiting arms. The child clung to her neck, weeping. When Asriel reached for the girl, she told him, "Mezana saved me."

Asriel smiled and turned to Mezana. "See, you do have a purpose," he said, indicating the child. "But you must always wear my shoes of peace. It's the only way you can avoid injury as you walk with me in difficult places and as you reach out to rescue those who are lost."

The Allegory Explained

Not only did Mezana's sandals allow her to complete a difficult course over broken shards of pottery, they also enabled her to rescue a young girl from the evil clutches of Beliah. The sandals of God's peace give us the same kind of powers; God's peace not only protects us as we travel rough roads, it helps us complete our calling to rescue the lost.

When we wear our shoes of peace, we can travel any road Jesus calls us to. We can do this because he is with us.

Jesus promised us, "And I will ask the Father, and he shall give you another Comforter, that he may abide with you for ever, even the Spirit of truth, whom the world cannot receive because it does not see him, or know him; but ye know him, for he dwells with you and shall be in you" (John 14:16–17 JUB).

Just as God's Spirit rested inside the temple's Holy of Holies, it also rested on Jesus, and it now rests on us, making us living, breathing temples of God. The apostle Paul in 1 Corinthians 3:16 made this clear when he asked, "Don't you know that you are God's temple and that God's Spirit lives in you?" (GW).

If you think about it, this truth is so awesome, so wonderful, that it's almost beyond our human comprehension. God's very Spirit rests on us and is in us. When we understand this, we can rest in God's powerful peace.

This peace helps us in many ways. When we yield to God's peace, it heals our pain. It comforts us. It banishes fear so we can tell the good news that can rescue our friends and loved ones from the evil one. It reminds us that God is with us and we are never alone.

Paul's Run-In with a Slave Girl

When the apostle Paul and his missionary partner Silas rescued a slave girl from a demonic spirit, her masters were furious. After all, the girl had made them a good living as a demon-powered fortune-teller.

The ruckus started when the slave girl began following Paul and Silas everywhere they went, shouting, "These men are servants of the Most High God. They're telling you how you can be saved" (Acts 16:17 GW).

You'd think the two men would have appreciated her words. Surely she was helping them draw a crowd. But she was also drawing unwanted attention from the authorities and creating a distraction that kept the people from hearing the good news of Jesus. Paul finally told the evil spirit, "I command you in the name of Jesus Christ to come out of her!" (Acts 16:18 GW).

I doubt Paul and Silas realized the consequences of this action, as we read in Acts 16:19–24:

> When her owners realized that their hope of making money was gone, they grabbed Paul and Silas and dragged them to the authorities in the public square. In front of the Roman officials, they said, "These men are stirring up a lot of trouble in our city. They're Jews, and they're advocating customs that we can't accept or practice as Roman citizens."
> The crowd joined in the attack against Paul and Silas. Then the officials tore the clothes off Paul and Silas and ordered the guards to beat them with sticks. After they had hit Paul and Silas many times, they threw them in jail and ordered the jailer to keep them under tight security. So the jailer followed these orders and put Paul and Silas into solitary confinement with their feet in leg irons. (GW)

Things didn't look so good for Paul and Silas. Here they were in a strange town filled with people who wanted them dead. So how do you suppose they spent their evening? Did the two poison each other with complaints about the injustice of it all? Believe it or not, Paul and Silas allowed the peace of God to rule the night. Instead of complaining, they praised God. "Around midnight Paul and Silas were praying and singing hymns of praise to God. The other prisoners were listening to them" (Acts 16:25 GW).

How could they be so peaceful when so many things were going wrong? For all they knew, they could be facing execution at dawn. The peace of God kept them calm. The peace of God took away their bitterness. The peace of God gave them a thankful heart.

And how did God respond to Paul and Silas's faithful expression of peace? He sent an earthquake that opened the prison door and sprung the men from their chains.

You would think these two men would have made a break for it. But Paul and Silas stuck around. They were there when the jailer decided to fall on his own sword because he was sure his prisoners had escaped. Paul shouted, "Don't hurt yourself! We're all here!" (Acts 16:28 GW).

The jailer was so grateful that he invited Paul and Silas to spend the rest of the evening in his home. The jailer bandaged his guests' wounds and fed them a meal while he heard the good news of Jesus. That night the jailer and his entire family were saved, receiving Jesus as their Lord and Savior.

To start this town's church, Paul and Silas had to "walk across shards" in their shoes of peace. By that I mean they had to endure hardship while staying in the peace of God in order to share the Good News of Jesus with the jailer and his family.

Walking in peace not only helps us spread the Good News but also helps us live a holy life, as Hebrews 12:14 explains: "Work at living in peace with everyone, and work at living a holy life, for those who are not holy will not see the Lord" (NLT). Just as Paul and Silas kept peace with their jailer, we must keep peace with those God puts into our lives.

Lloyd John Ogilvie told this story:

One morning recently, as the Holy Spirit was equipping me with the whole armor and I was mentally putting on the shoes of peace, He reminded me of a resentment I had carried for several days. It was keeping me from feeling at peace. A friend had hurt me deeply, foolishly I had nursed the resentment. That morning I'd asked the Holy Spirit to counsel me on what to do. In the quiet, as I put on the shoes of peace, He showed me that I had to surrender my resentment and forgive the man. "Do it now," the Spirit seemed to say. "Then go to him and tell him you have forgiven him." I followed the Spirit's orders and peace flooded my heart again.[4]

Paul may have been hotheaded at times, but he often demonstrated the power of peace. He also taught it, as we can see in the conclusion to a letter he wrote to the church at Thessalonica.

Brothers and sisters, we ask you to show your appreciation for those leaders who work among you and instruct you. We ask you to love them and think very highly of them because of the work they are doing. Live in peace with each other.

We encourage you, brothers and sisters, to instruct those who are not living right, cheer up those who are discouraged, help the weak, and be patient with everyone. Make sure that no one ever pays back one wrong with another wrong. Instead, always try to do what is good for each other and everyone else.

Always be joyful. Never stop praying. Whatever happens, give thanks, because it is God's will in Christ Jesus that you do this.

Don't put out the Spirit's fire. Don't despise what God has revealed. Instead, test everything. Hold on to what is good. Keep away from every kind of evil. (1 Thess. 5:12–22 GW)

These are great and fitting words of peace, fitting also for us.

The Armor

The sandals worn by Roman soldiers were made from thick leather, and the bottoms of the sandals were covered with hobnails to create traction, making it easy for the soldiers to scramble over sharp rocks.

But it was more than sharp rocks the Roman army had to worry about. Lloyd John Ogilvie explained it like this:

Often in the field where the Roman soldiers met an enemy for battle, there would be short, sharp spears protruding from the ground, hidden in among the grass so the soldiers couldn't see them. As the soldiers marched on, their feet would be pierced unless they had thick-soled shoes. I believe that some of this is what Paul had in mind when he described shoeing our feet with the preparation of the gospel of peace.[5]

We may not be in the Roman army, but we are in the service of Jesus Christ. We too have marching orders. How much peace will we have if we follow our orders barefoot? Our bare soles will feel every briar and thorn, every sharp pebble and shard of glass, every protruding spear tip and sun-broiled stone. If we are spiritually barefoot, the journey could leave us crippled. We need to shod our feet with the peace of Jesus. When we travel with the gospel of peace, we travel with the presence of God, who continually leads us to his purposes.

Suiting Up

One day I was walking the dog and praying when (in my mind's eye) I saw myself being superimposed with Christ. It was as if I was wearing him. It was a powerful moment for me as I saw that I was "in" Christ. This concept helps us realize the importance of placing our feet inside of Christ's so we go with him and in him as we walk the path of purpose.

We need to keep in mind that walking in God's purposes will attract the attention of our enemy. So does this mean we should sit on the fence so that we don't attract the enemy's attention? No, it means we should get ready for battle. Lysa TerKeurst said, "When you seek to serve others, you are doing the Father's will. Satan hates those who jump off the fence of complacency and start making a real difference for Christ. You will be on the front lines of the battle and in need of your armor more than ever before."[6]

Have you ever been in a hurry to make it to an appointment when one of your shoes went missing? You looked in all the likely places—the bottom of your closet, under the bed, beneath the couch—but the shoe was nowhere! If this scenario has ever happened to you, you know how important it is for that shoe to be found because shoes are often required for our most important appointments. For example, you wouldn't go to a job interview barefoot or wearing only one good shoe. Just as prospective employers could lose sight of your potential if you showed up for an interview without shoes, you can lose sight of your potential if you forget to wear the peace that passes understanding.

If this should happen, don't panic. Ask for the light of God's truth to show you where you left your peace, then ask for the power of God's Holy Spirit to help you reshod your feet.

> *Dear Lord,*
>
> *If I have lost my peace, show me where I left it. If I discarded it because of trauma, I command the spirit of trauma to leave me in the name of Jesus. I ask, Lord, that you replace my trauma with your peace, with the knowing that in you everything is going to be okay. In fact, I put on your shoes of peace, inviting your Spirit to walk with me, to be in me. Knowing that you are with me gives me peaceful courage to go wherever you want to send me. I am in your service. Lead me to your purposes in your peace. In Jesus's name, amen.*

ARMORED RESPONSE

If we want to wear the shoes of peace well, we may need to take off a few stinky socks, such as strife, anger, and jealousy.

Strife-Fighting Scripture

"He who is of a proud heart stirs up strife, but he who trusts in the LORD will be prospered" (Prov. 28:25 NKJV).

Declaration to Defeat Strife

I declare that I lay down my pride at the feet of Jesus. I humble myself before him, trusting in him. I declare that because I am trusting in Jesus, I do not have to lose my peace with others.

Prayer for Victory over Strife

Dear Lord,

Forgive me for allowing my pride and lack of trust in you to pull me out of your peace. Help me to stand against injustice in the strength of your peace.

Anger-Fighting Scripture

"Remember this, my dear brothers and sisters: Everyone should be quick to listen, slow to speak, and should not get angry easily. An angry person doesn't do what God approves of" (James 1:19–20 GW).

Declaration to Defeat Anger

I declare that, through the peace of God, I will be quick to listen, slow to speak, and slow to become angry so that I can live my life in the approval of God.

Prayer for Victory over Anger

Dear Lord,

I tell the spirit of anger to leave in the name and authority of Jesus. In its place, I ask that you give me your Spirit of peace. In that peace, help me to follow after your purpose for my life.

Jealousy-Fighting Scripture

"But if you are bitterly jealous and filled with self-centered ambition, don't brag. Don't say that you are wise when it isn't true. That kind of wisdom doesn't come from above. It belongs to this world. It is self-centered and demonic. Wherever there is jealousy and rivalry, there is disorder and every kind of evil" (James 3:14–16 GW).

Declaration to Defeat Jealousy

I lay down my envy at the feet of Jesus, trading it for his peace. I declare that I will trust God in all things.

Prayer for Victory over Jealousy

Dear Lord,

Forgive me for tinkering with the demonic whenever I've chosen to envy or follow selfish ambition instead of following and trusting you. In your name, I cast out any spirit of selfish ambition and envy in me and trade it for your peace that passes understanding. Give me your peace and your strength to trust you as my provider and to trust that you are with me in all things. In Jesus's name, amen.

6

Wielding the Shield of Faith

In addition to all of these, hold up the shield of faith to stop
the fiery arrows of the devil.

Ephesians 6:16 NLT

I'm involved with a prayer team. As we pray over the people
who drop in to see us after church, we ask the Lord to show us
how to minister to each of our guests. One rainy morning my
friend Terri and I were praying over Beth, a beautiful young
woman we'd only just met. As we prayed, Terri and I could
feel Beth was struggling with fear. Terri asked to borrow my
red umbrella and told Beth, "God's protection over us is like
this red umbrella." She pushed a button on the handle, and
the umbrella popped open. Terri stood beneath the umbrella
and invited us to stand with her. She said, "As long as we stand
beneath this umbrella, we are protected from the rain. When
we stand beneath the shield of faith, Jesus's blood protects
us from the enemy."

The three of us huddled beneath the umbrella as we continued to pray for Beth. I told Beth, "I don't know what you do, but I feel God wants you to know that though evil is watching you, you are protected by the Word. The Word is above you, around you, beneath you. The Word is Jesus."

Beth soon shared that she belonged to a small group of women who go into brothels up and down the highways to rescue trafficked girls. She told us she and her friends pray the Word, then walk into these dark places and walk out with rescued girls in tow. Beth said, "The safeguards other groups use don't work for us. We rely on the Word and get miraculous results."

When Beth goes on these rescue missions, she may be afraid, but she activates her shield of faith by quickening her faith through the power of the Word of God. When she quickens her faith, the blood of Jesus becomes her shield and she is able to walk into the enemy's camp and steal their "merchandise," young girls she and her friends lead to freedom.

What a great example of what it's like to wield the shield of faith, which deflects against the arrows of the enemy. When we carry our shield, we can escape harm, even when we're called to raid the enemy's camp.

Our Quest

Paul recommended that we seek the protection of the shield of faith when he said, "In addition to all of these, hold up the shield of faith to stop the fiery arrows of the devil" (Eph. 6:16 NLT).

We need to be protected from the fiery darts of the enemy so we can accomplish the purposes God calls us to. We find strength to accomplish our purposes when we deepen our faith in God. J. Dwight Pentecost, a distinguished professor of Bible exposition at Dallas Theological Seminary, explained, "Strength in the Christian life is Jesus Christ. Power in the Christian life is Jesus Christ. We may appropriate that strength and power by faith."[1]

Beth and her friends cannot rescue girls without lifting up their shield of faith. God is their leader. He is their power. He is also their strength and protection. It's a supernatural arrangement.

My dear friend, author and speaker Thelma Wells, puts it this way:

> Without faith it is impossible to please God and spiritual victory won't happen. Faith is the substance of things hoped for. Faith assures us that God hears and answers our prayers. Faith sparks our hope in the healing power of God. Faith gives us the assurance that we will have what we need to live. Faith helps us hold on to the promises of God when things look bleak. Faith helps us deal with changes in climate and uncertainties of life. Faith helps us lean on the everlasting arms of God when all around us is crashing. Faith reaches beyond what we can see and gives us encouragement that life will work out in the future.[2]

Mezana's Quest

Before Asriel left Mezana's home, he put his hand on the little girl's head. "Mezana, could you look after Cara for me?"

"This is one of my purposes, is it not?" Mezana asked as she reached for the child, who filled her arms with a joyful hug.

Asriel nodded and took Mezana's hand. "It's also a great responsibility. You will need to be prepared."

"What are you saying?"

"As you know, this city is at war with the evil one."

Mezana felt fear almost buckle her legs as she and Cara studied Asriel's face.

"Are we in danger then?"

"Beware of the fiery arrows," Asriel warned. "They could fall from the sky when you least expect them. That's why I do not want you to go anywhere in town without your shield."

"Shield?"

Asriel pointed to the largest shield Mezana had ever seen.

"That looks heavy," Mezana said.

"Not when you carry it in my strength. Promise me you'll be careful, okay? An attack is imminent."

After Asriel left, Mezana said to Cara, "Let's grab our shield and hurry to the market so we can purchase fresh food for tonight's dinner." But when Mezana tried to pick up the shield, she was amazed at its size. If it weren't for Asriel's warning, she was sure she would have discarded it as too bulky.

Soon Mezana trudged down the road with the shield as Cara followed behind. Mezana was surprised at the number of people she passed who also carried the shield of Asriel. So she wasn't the only one he'd instructed to be on the lookout.

When she and Cara arrived at the market, she tried to balance the shield in her grip as she reached to inspect an onion.

"Your shield looks heavy," a familiar voice told her.

Mezana could not see the owner of the voice through her shield, but she answered anyway. "Mainly awkward."

"Why don't you leave your shield here next to my vegetable stand? That way you can finish your shopping with ease."

Mezana peered from behind the shield and was surprised to see Beliah grinning back at her.

"You work here in the market?"

"I am everywhere," Beliah said with a laugh. "But do not fear. I am unarmed."

Beliah pointed at a number of shields resting against his stand. "Besides, this is a safe place."

"Not with you here."

"You hurt my feelings, Mezana. Do you think I would attack you in this busy place?"

An old woman, one of Beliah's customers, tapped Mezana on the shoulder. "I leave my shield here all the time. Nothing's ever happened to me."

"Just for a moment then," Mezana said as she leaned her shield next to the others. Soon she and Cara were caught in the crowd, moving from booth to booth as they bartered for bread and eggs.

Zumpth! A burning arrow fell from the sky, landing at their feet. Cara screamed, and Mezana grabbed her hand as a rider of the evil one galloped toward them on a black stallion. Mezana pulled Cara along as they ran back to the booth where she'd left her shield.

Beliah blocked her. "Looking for something?" he asked mockingly.

Fear rose in Mezana, and she staggered backward, realizing she and Cara would soon be prisoners of the evil one unless she could get to her shield.

"In the name of Asriel, step aside," she demanded.

To her amazement, the giant of a man before her appeared to shrivel.

"Why should I?" he challenged, unaware he was losing his evil power.

"Because I command you to do so in the name of Asriel!"

Zumpth! A flaming arrow struck the vegetable stand, and it burst into flames.

Mezana pushed past the shrinking Beliah and grabbed her shield. She pulled Cara beside her as they knelt beneath it. "We'll be safe here," she told the girl.

Zumpth! A burning arrow struck her shield but bounced off without piercing it or setting it ablaze.

Then just as suddenly as the raid started, it was over. When Mezana and Cara lifted the shield, they saw that Beliah and the horseman were gone.

As they walked back to their home, they passed a lifeless victim of the attack, the old woman who had coaxed them to leave their shield behind.

"Such a shame she was caught without her shield," a town-woman said as they passed.

A man cried, "And my daughter too! She was taken by the horseman!"

Mezana shivered, glad they had escaped such a fate by using her shield before it was too late.

The Allegory Explained

Like Mezana, we must always be aware that we are at war with the evil one. We must be willing to wield our faith wherever we go, no matter how awkward it may seem. Otherwise arrows will take us unaware. Fear, discouragement, lack, injustice, lies, anger, and slander are all flaming arrows that will pierce our hearts if we are not prepared for Satan's attacks.

The only way we can survive these onslaughts is by using our shield of faith. This means having the knowledge that no matter what is happening we can trust God. It means believing that God himself surrounds us like a shield, as Psalm 5:11–12 describes: "But let all who take refuge in you be glad; let them ever sing for joy. Spread your protection over them, that those who love your name may rejoice in you. Surely, LORD, you bless the righteous; you surround them with your favor as with a shield."

The Apostle Paul and the Lame Man

One of the ways the disciples helped to grow the church after Jesus's resurrection and ascension into heaven was by praying for the sick and lame in the name of Jesus. These prayers for healing were effective because of the disciples' access to the power of the Holy Spirit.

Does God still heal today? Some would say no, but I've seen it happen many times. Of course, many factors come into play when healing is involved, but the most important factor is faith.

As a person who is often asked to pray for the sick, I can tell you miracles can happen when the person who is being prayed for has faith. For example, I recently prayed for a woman in chronic pain. She believed she would be healed, and suddenly, she was healed. After our time of prayer, she bent down to pick up her purse and shouted, "I have no pain!"

"What do you mean?" I asked.

"I couldn't pick up my purse without pain, but now I can! Jesus has healed me!"

I rejoiced with her, for she had received healing as she'd caught hold of faith.

There are times I wish I was better at catching hold of faith, for when I catch hold of it, I see God move in miraculous ways. When I don't catch hold of it and begin to doubt or overanalyze, I do not see God move as readily. It's as simple as that.

The apostle Paul understood this concept. In the book of Acts, we see what happened when he encountered a cripple who suddenly "caught" the faith he needed to be healed.

> While they were at Lystra, Paul and Barnabas came upon a man with crippled feet. He had been that way from birth, so he had never walked. He was sitting and listening as Paul preached. Looking straight at him, Paul realized he had faith to be healed. So Paul called to him in a loud voice, "Stand up!" And the man jumped to his feet and started walking. (14:8–10 NLT)

I have never seen a cripple healed, and if I did, I would be filled with joy. Imagine it! But Paul didn't have to imagine it; he saw it. He shared the truth of the Word of God, the man believed, and then Paul told him to stand and he did. That's faith, on the part of both Paul and the man who was healed.

Is faith really that simple? It is. Faith is simply believing that God is willing and able. Hebrews 11:1 says, "Faith is the confidence that what we hope for will actually happen; it gives us assurance about things we cannot see" (NLT).

In many ways, faith is something we carry like a shield.

The Armor

Imagine what it was like to be a Roman soldier, lugging a huge shield everywhere you went.

The young Roman soldier knelt on one knee and crouched behind the three-and-a half-foot-tall wooden shield. Thunk! A flaming arrow soaked in pitch bounced off the shield and fell to the ground. If the fiery pitch had stuck to his armor, it would have made it red hot.

Miles earlier, this soldier had secretly begrudged his captain for making him carry this twenty-two-pound wooden shield covered in layers of leather. His shield, the size of a small door, had been a burden on the march, but now, as yet another arrow bounced harmlessly away, he was glad for its protection. He was also glad that he had soaked his shield in water, another way to keep the flaming arrows of the enemy from catching his shield on fire.

The soldier had to kneel in order to be protected. So must we. Our faith, after all, is in God through his Word and the work of the shed blood of Jesus. When we kneel to God in prayer, we are activating our faith. As David said in Psalm 7:10, "God is my shield, saving those whose hearts are true and right" (NLT).

Roman shields had yet another secret. These shields allowed the soldiers to become as one. The soldiers could overlap their shields and advance in a large group against an opposing army or lift their overlapping shields to the sky to stop a hail of flaming arrows.

How wonderful it is to know that we can combine our faith and prayers with those of other believers to create an even stronger defense against the enemy.

Suiting Up

Do we need a shield of faith today? More than ever!

Author Kay Arthur wrote:

> Girding yourself with truth is not enough. You need a shield of faith to counteract the enemy's offense. When you use specific truths from God's Word to counteract the devil's lies and accusations, you're taking up the shield of faith! It is a defensive action! When the enemy attacks, the shield extinguishes the lie or accusation with an appropriate truth or promise that you've chosen to believe. Apparently there's not a single lie or accusation we can't extinguish. God says we will be able to extinguish all the flaming missiles of the evil one! That's awesome isn't it! If we get burned, it's because we didn't construct a shield that was big enough or because we didn't soak it with enough water. Shields can dry out so you must be in the Word day by day.[3]

We need to remember that our shield of faith is soaked in both the Word and the blood of Jesus. Thelma Wells says, "Praise the Lord we don't have to live unprotected any longer! We've got the blood of Jesus, the love of Jesus, the hope in Jesus, the restoration of Jesus, and the total covering by Him for our heads, hearts, minds, feet, and back. We can stand strong in the midst of turmoil, ready to fight the good fight of faith without fear."[4]

To take up the shield of faith, we must first take up the Bible and open it. We must hold on to the treasures we find within its pages. When we have faith that God's Word is true and that Christ's blood washed away our sins, our faith is like a shield of protection against the enemy.

> *Dear Lord,*
> *There are so many wonderful Scripture passages I can hide behind when the enemy sends a fiery arrow my way. I choose to have faith in your Word. I believe that your Son covers me with his blood so that I can know and walk with you and do your good purposes. Thank you that you are the author and finisher of my faith and that my faith in you will shield me from every firestorm. Help me to always carry this shield you have so graciously given me. In Jesus's name, amen.*

ARMORED RESPONSE

That was a really strong prayer, and to follow it up, we are going to pray against unbelief and doubt, enemies of faith.

Unbelief-Fighting Scripture

"I do believe; help me overcome my unbelief!" (Mark 9:24).

Declaration to Defeat Unbelief

I declare that I believe in the truth of Jesus Christ. I believe that I can be in his truth and that his truth can be in me. I believe I can buckle his truth around me like a belt to dispel all the lies of the enemy. I believe Jesus can turn my unbelief into belief in him.

Prayer for Victory over Unbelief

Dear Lord,

Forgive me for allowing any unbelief into my heart, for I choose to believe in you. Teach me how to believe and help me keep my trust in you.

Doubt-Fighting Scripture

"Then Jesus told them, 'I tell you the truth, if you have faith and don't doubt, you can do things like this and much more. You can even say to this mountain, "May you be lifted up and thrown into the sea," and it will happen'" (Matt. 21:21 NLT).

Declaration to Defeat Doubt

I declare that I believe the words of Jesus, who told the truth. I believe that if I do not doubt, I can do all things God has called me to do through Christ. I can tell my mountains to move, and they will move.

Prayer for Victory over Doubt

Dear Lord,

Forgive me for doubting you or the call you have given me. I ask that you erase my doubt and give me the vision of what it means to have faith. Give me the ability to say that I believe and to tell my mountains to move. Thank you for your faithfulness, Lord. In Jesus's name, amen.

7

Wearing the Helmet of Salvation

Put on salvation as your helmet.

Ephesians 6:17 NLT

My friend Dianne Butts and her husband, Hal, decided to follow the path of a motorcycle ride for fallen police officers so they could pray over the event and its riders at various stops along the way. Hal was on his Harley motorcycle, while Dianne rode her Kawasaki Nomad 1500cc. After lunch in Castle Rock, Colorado, the couple, along with their friend Margi, decided to head south on I-25 to Pueblo. The three riders were all wearing their motorcycle helmets, something Hal, a retired state trooper, always insisted upon. As they drove down the interstate at 75 miles per hour, Hal rode ahead of Dianne, with Margi riding rear guard. Just behind Margi was a truck pulling a camper.

As the motorcycle group headed south, Dianne suddenly felt as though she'd hit a headwind. She thought it odd because the nearby trees were as still as sentries, guarding the road without rustling a leaf. Yet when she checked her speedometer, she had slowed down to 65 miles per hour.

Because of Dianne's slower speed, the truck behind Margi pulled into the left-hand passing lane to go around the motorcyclists. That's when Dianne's bike started to shimmy and pull to the left. She was veering too close to the white line, to the passing truck and camper! She tried to pull her bike back to the right, but instead her bike swerved to the left, and Dianne plowed right into the camper with her shoulder. She felt herself lift off her bike, which disappeared as Dianne began to roll sideways down the highway. With her eyes open, she watched the pavement go by again and again and again. All she could do was pray, "Jesus!"

Dianne later explained that this prayer contained everything in her heart. "Jesus, I'm helpless. I'm out of control. Please give me your hand!"

Finally, Dianne came to a stop, and all she could hear was silence. That's when she realized she was still on the highway. She knew an eighteen-wheeler could plow her down at any moment, so painfully she began to crawl toward the side of the road, sliding on her side and one elbow. Being a former EMT, Dianne began to assess her injuries. Her hands were swollen, but she could wiggle her toes. She could also think, so these were good signs. Hal hadn't seen the accident and had driven on down the road, but Margi had pulled her bike to the side of the road and came running.

By the time Hal was able to turn around and come back through the now heavy traffic, the ambulance had arrived. The EMTs loaded Dianne on a stretcher along with her full-face helmet, something the doctors always want to see when they evaluate a motorcyclist's injuries.

In the end, Dianne survived a 65-mile-an-hour plunge onto the concrete. The result was a totaled bike, a chipped ankle, a seriously skinned elbow requiring stitches, deep bruises on her legs, and a terrible case of road rash on her bare arms that was comparable to serious burns. But no head injury! When the ER doctor examined Dianne's full-face helmet, she commented, "If this patient hadn't been wearing this helmet today, she wouldn't have a face."[1]

This accident, caused by the sudden deflation of Dianne's front tire, could have been fatal. But Dianne's life was spared mainly because she was wearing her motorcycle helmet, a lesson that serves as a great parallel to our study on the helmet of salvation.

The helmet of salvation saves us not only from the enemy's mental oppressions but also from hell through the grace of Jesus. If it weren't for the helmet of salvation, we would never receive the crown of life. And we could never receive the crown of life if Jesus hadn't worn his crown of thorns, faced death, and been resurrected from the grave.

New York Times bestselling author Mark Batterson pointed out the importance of Jesus's work when he said, "When Jesus rose from the dead, it radically redefined reality. When He walked out of the tomb under His own power, the word *impossible* was removed from our vocabulary. The resurrection is the history-changer, the game-changer. But the trick is learning to live as if Jesus was crucified yesterday, rose from the dead today, and is coming back tomorrow."[2]

The first step to accomplishing this trick is to put on the helmet of salvation.

Our Quest

Paul tells us to "put on salvation as your helmet" (Eph. 6:17 NLT). The helmet of salvation reminds us that we belong to God and that we can have the mind of Christ. With this assurance, we can have the confidence to venture into his purposes for us.

So how do we wear the helmet of salvation well?

The first order of business is to put it on. It's the best way to enjoy its beautifying effects. Psalm 149:4 says, "For the LORD takes pleasure in His people; He will beautify the humble with salvation" (NKJV). Beautify? Absolutely. It's as Charles Spurgeon, a preacher from the 1800s, once said: "To the eyes of Jesus we are radiant with beauty because God has loved us."[3]

Second, we must use the helmet of salvation to remind us that we belong to Christ and are saved by grace. But why is this great love directed at us in the first place? Back to the words of Spurgeon: "Jesus loves us because we belong to the Father, and the Father loves us because we belong to Jesus."[4]

Third, we must allow our helmet of salvation to protect our thought life. J. Dwight Pentecost explained, "The thought life determines whether [the child of God] experiences victory or defeat."[5] If we follow the wrong thoughts, we will fulfill the wrong purposes.

And speaking of wrong thoughts, in an episode of the comic strip *Dilbert*, a cartoon about office nerds, Dilbert creates a brain stimulator that he wears like a headband on his rather large head. But the stimulator malfunctions, causing him to kill a coworker in the break room. While being arrested, Dilbert professes his innocence while admitting the guilt of his cyborg parts. In other words, Dilbert is admitting that an outside force caused him to lose control.[6]

I think we've heard this before in the "Twinkie Defense," when in 1979, a defendant named Dan White claimed he'd murdered two men, including the mayor of San Francisco, because he'd eaten nothing but junk food and in so doing had caused his mood to go out of sync.

Are you buying that? The jury did, lessening White's sentence from premeditated murder to manslaughter, a decision that created riots in the streets.

That said, let me pose a question to you. Can the enemy serve as an evil brain stimulator or a bad mood modifier? Sure he can. After all, Satan is the great deceiver who loves to whisper lies, create misunderstandings, and hand you thoughts that not only depress you but also cause you to do irrational things, things you would never think, say, or do when you've activated "the mind of Christ" (1 Cor. 2:16).

Wearing the helmet of salvation will help us look good, enjoy a saving relationship with God, and activate the mind of Christ. This is good news.

Mezana's Quest

Days after the attack on their village, Cara came to Mezana with a wonderful idea. "Let's take our fishing poles down to the shore to catch tonight's dinner."

Mezana couldn't resist the suggestion on such a beautiful afternoon. Besides, they had been cooped up for days.

Mezana grabbed her shield, and soon the pair was scrambling along a secluded outcropping of rocks that rose over the sparkling sea. They discovered a hidden cove, and it wasn't long before Cara and Mezana were dangling their lines in the water as they enjoyed the peace of the late afternoon. After a while, Mezana caught sight of her reflection.

Her hair! Her hair was longer since her rescue, but she still wore the brutally jagged cut that signified she was a slave. Mezana felt heat prickle her cheeks, embarrassed that everyone who saw her knew her shame.

She shielded her watering eyes from the sudden glare of the setting sun. Her heart skipped a beat. How had it gotten so late?

The darkness was already fingering its way through the sky and across the water toward her with its taunting whispers. "Why did Asriel choose you? You never deserved him. You don't deserve him now. He will soon see what you are and abandon you to be a slave again."

Mezana shivered and pulled her line from the water. It was time to go. Past time. But when she turned to find Cara, the child was nowhere to be seen.

Mezana grabbed their things and scrambled over the rocks. "Cara! Where are you?" she called as she raced down the beach.

The whispering voices answered her panic. "Cara's been taken because you neglected her. You have failed Asriel. You will never be able to face him again."

"Cara! Cara!" Mezana called as the whispers grew louder in the evening breeze.

Falling on her knees weeping, Mezana did the only thing she could think of. She called out for Asriel. "Please help me!"

"Mezana!"

Mezana looked up to see Asriel walking toward her, hand in hand with Cara.

Mezana rose from the sand and rushed to meet them. "Cara, I was so worried!"

"Didn't you know I was walking with Asriel?"

Mezana knelt and hugged the girl. "I thought you were taken."

"But I told you I was with him. Didn't you hear me?"

"The dark whispers must have drowned out your voice," Mezana said.

Cara nodded her head. "I heard them too and was frightened. That's why Asriel came to me."

Asriel told the pair, "I have a gift for the two of you down by the fire."

Soon Mezana and Cara were perched on driftwood and enjoying the fire's glowing warmth as Asriel roasted the fish they'd caught for dinner. The firelight reflected in Cara's bright eyes as she asked Asriel, "Didn't you say you brought us presents?"

Asriel smiled and handed Cara and Mezana two lovely wrapped packages. When Mezana opened hers, she gasped. It was a woven cap of golden thread. "It's beautiful," she said. She placed the cap on her head. It fit perfectly. Now no one would see her shame because her shorn head was wonderfully covered. She turned and helped Cara tuck her locks inside her own golden cap. It too was a perfect fit.

Cara stared at Mezana. "You look so beautiful!"

Mezana smiled down at the child. "As do you."

Asriel told them, "My gift signifies that I have saved you and that you are under my protection. When you wear your cap, you will be identified as mine and will not be mistaken for slaves of the evil one."

Cara pulled the cap over her ears and exclaimed, "Mezana, can you hear the dark whispers now?"

Mezana pulled her cap low and listened before answering in awe, "The whispers of the darkness are gone!"

Asriel laughed. "And so they are! As long as you wear your gift and remember to whom you belong, you will not be able to hear the whispers and lies of the darkness. And if you do, you will not be enticed to believe them."

"Thank you!" Cara cried. "The dark whispers scared me. They mocked me and told me I was an orphan no one could love."

Asriel took Cara's hand and joined it with Mezana's.

"That, my dear child, is a terrible lie," he said, "for darkness always lies. The truth is you have been adopted into my kingdom for my good purposes. You now walk in my love."

The Allegory Explained

I love the picture of Asriel giving Cara and Mezana their golden hats, representing how Jesus gives us the helmet of salvation. As Paul explained in 1 Thessalonians 5:8, "But let us who live in the light be clearheaded, protected by the armor of faith and love, and wearing as our helmet the confidence of our salvation" (NLT).

When we put on the helmet of salvation, we are clearheaded. The evil whispers and lies of the darkness will fade away into nothing. Jesus said in John 8:12, "I am the light of the world. If you follow me, you won't have to walk in darkness, because you will have the light that leads to life" (NLT).

Paul in Rome

Ah, Rome, the capital city of the Roman Empire, a city of four million people, and a place where Paul often observed the armor of the Roman soldiers who were assigned to guard him.

Paul's visit to Rome did not follow an easy path. He had been imprisoned in Jerusalem and shipwrecked in Malta. But while Paul was under house arrest in Rome, awaiting his trial before Caesar, he wrote the epistles of Ephesians, Philippians, Colossians, and Philemon.

In his writings, he explained joy to the Philippians and the armor of God to the Ephesians, and all the while he continued to explain the mystery of salvation, just as he did in Ephesians 1:7–8: "He is so rich in kindness and grace that he purchased our freedom with the blood of his Son and forgave our sins. He has showered his kindness on us, along with all wisdom and understanding" (NLT).

If Paul had not been imprisoned in Rome, it's possible our Bibles would not contain these wonderful and crucial books. Perhaps Paul's greater purpose through his troubles was to write down these powerful revelations, including his revelations about salvation, so we would know how to be saved.

The Armor

If we were able to view a Roman soldier's helmet, as Paul did, we would see that it was either a molded metal cap or a cap made of leather covered with metal scales. The helmet was worn to prevent the soldier from having his skull split open by a crash of a broadsword.

Orlando Magic executive and author Pat Williams commented on this piece of armor by saying:

> Any soldier who goes into battle without his helmet is taking a foolish risk. A helmet covers the head, protecting the brain, the organ of thought. The helmet of salvation guards the warrior's thoughts and his will; it preserves his life. When the enemy attacks and tries to disrupt our thoughts and corrupt our will, we can rely on our salvation to repel those attacks: "No matter how difficult my circumstances, no matter how I feel emotionally, no matter how Satan may attack me, I *know* that Jesus Christ is saving me right now. I put my trust in my helmet of my salvation."[7]

But the most beautiful thing about the helmet of salvation is that we don't have to purchase it ourselves because Jesus, who already paid the price, freely gives it to us. We don't even have to earn our salvation by fulfilling our purposes; fulfilling our purposes is just another bonus of following Christ. Ephesians 2:8–10 says, "God saved you by his grace when you believed. And you can't take credit for this; it is a gift from God. Salvation is not a reward for the good things we have done, so none of us can boast about it. For we are God's masterpiece. He has created us anew in Christ Jesus, so we can do the good things he planned for us long ago" (NLT).

Suiting Up

As we put on the helmet of salvation, we naturally remove a few filthy rags, including "sexual immorality, impurity, lustful pleasures, idolatry, sorcery, hostility, quarreling, jealousy, outbursts of anger, selfish ambition, dissension, division, envy, drunkenness, wild parties, and other sins like these" (Gal. 5:19–21 NLT), and we clothe ourselves in Jesus. This transformation comes with our salvation and is accomplished through the power of the Holy Spirit, who also gives us the fruit of "love, joy, peace, not giving up, being kind, being good, having faith, being gentle, and being the boss over our own desires" (Gal. 5:22–23 NLV).

Each of us has to engage the truth that Jesus is our Savior and that he is saving us. Pastor and author Charles Stanley explained, "Nobody can make you think, God is in the process of saving me right now! You have to choose to think that thought in every negative situation, in every troublesome moment, and in every painful and traumatic experience."[8]

He continued by saying:

I heard the story about a young woman who was mugged on a city street and was on the verge of being raped at knifepoint. She kept saying repeatedly to herself and to her assailant, "Jesus is my Savior. Jesus is my Savior. Jesus is my Savior." The man became so troubled by what she was saying that he eventually released her and ran from her.

Now such a statement is not a magic formula to use in a time of trouble, but, my friend, such a statement is a declaration of the truth. We do well to remind ourselves often, "Jesus is my Savior!" We do well to say to others, "Jesus is my Savior! He desires to be your Savior too."[9]

Wise words from Stanley. Now let's pray.

Dear Lord,

Thank you that you are my Savior! Thank you that through Jesus's work on the cross and his resurrection from the dead I belong to you. I give you my sins in exchange for your salvation, Lord. I wear this salvation as a helmet to remind me that you are not only saving me but also transforming me through the power of the Holy Spirit. Thank you that you are leading me to do good works that you planned for me long ago. In Jesus's name, amen.

ARMORED RESPONSE

One of the enemy's sneaky attacks against the joy of our salvation is to put us in the spiral of self-condemnation. So instead of celebrating all that Jesus has done for us through his saving grace, and instead of using that joy to propel us into the good works God has called us to do, we pull out a mirror to study our flaws. Yes, we all have flaws, but fixating on our flaws instead of the goodness of God will lead our hearts to believe we are still condemned. We must dispel this lie with Scripture.

Self-Condemnation–Fighting Scripture

"So those who are believers in Christ Jesus can no longer be condemned" (Rom. 8:1 GW).

Declaration to Defeat Self-Condemnation

I declare that Jesus is my Savior and that I am being transformed by the Holy Spirit. I am no longer condemned.

Prayer for Victory over Self-Condemnation

Dear Lord,

Forgive me for continuing to believe you condemn me, for you are not comparing me to Christ. You are looking at me through the righteousness of Christ. And if you no longer condemn me, how can I condemn myself? Help me not to see myself as unforgiven but as redeemed through the blood of Christ. Thank you! In Jesus's name, amen.

8

Brandishing the
Sword of the Spirit

Take the sword of the Spirit, which is the word of God.

Ephesians 6:17 NLT

My friend Roxanne was in a terrible car crash that left her
with injuries as well as mountains of medical bills. She had
no idea how she would pay her bills, but after much prayer,
she came up with a wonderful solution. She took a brown
paper bag and a marker and wrote the names of Jesus on the
bag, including the Word, Light of the World, Healer, Messiah,
Mighty One, Prince of Life, Savior of the World, Provider,
Truth, Shepherd, Son, Rabbi, Power of God, the Rock, Most
High God, and Word of Life.

Next, Roxanne took a sheet of paper and wrote down her
injuries, including her befuddling confusion from her brain
trauma. She tucked the list and her bills into the bag and

gave the entire bag to Jesus. "My bills and injuries belong to you, Jesus!"

Shortly thereafter, Roxanne's doctor gave her the name of a woman to call. Roxanne called her and told her about her car accident and not being able to pay her bills. That's when the woman took it upon herself to write to all the people to whom Roxanne owed money. Roxanne doesn't know what the woman wrote or even why she wrote. All Roxanne knows for sure is that one after the other her debtors forgave her debt.

Today Roxanne's debt is gone, and her injuries have been miraculously healed. I do not believe this was a lucky coincidence. I think Roxanne found the solution when she applied the name of Jesus to her situation. He is the one about whom it is written, "The Word (Christ) was in the beginning. The Word was with God. The Word was God. He was with God in the beginning. He made all things. Nothing was made without Him making it. Life began by Him. His Life was the Light for men. The Light shines in the darkness. The darkness has never been able to put out the Light" (John 1:1–5 NLV).[1]

Roxanne reached out to the Word. She touched the Word, and she trusted the Word. Then the Word, Jesus, supplied all her needs and healed all her infirmities because nothing is impossible with God (Luke 18:27).

What would happen if we all trusted the Word and stopped being afraid of his Spirit, the Holy Spirit?

Is the church today afraid of the power of the Holy Spirit? Well, yes, at least according to Paul. He says that in the last days people "will do things to make it look as if they are Christians. But they will not receive the power that is for a Christian. Keep away from such people" (2 Tim. 3:5 NLV).

We do not want to be people who resemble what the Word says but denies the power of the Spirit of God. We want to be people of purpose, brandishing the sword of the Spirit. Then we can move with strength, faith, power, and purpose.

Our Quest

Paul tells us to "take the sword of the Spirit, which is the word of God" (Eph. 6:17 NLT). The sword of the Spirit is God's Word ignited with the power of God's Spirit. Wielding this sword will empower us to fulfill our assignments and purposes with the Holy Spirit's power.

With this in mind, we must be on the lookout so that the enemy does not steal the Word from us. We can guard the Word by

- reading it (renewing our minds)
- thinking about it (meditating on it and memorizing it)
- praying it (putting it to work)
- keeping it at the center of our lives (not letting the enemy distract us from its power or purpose)
- honoring it (living our lives according to it)
- receiving its power (letting the Holy Spirit into our lives so that the Spirit ignites the Word)
- allowing it to guide us (using it as our compass)

Lysa TerKeurst warns, "Don't look to the world for your purpose. Look into God's Word. Let your mind be transformed day by day. This is part of our purpose—to get alone in the Word with our Master and seek His will every day.

Don't seek to fulfill this part of your purpose with details of the tasks to be completed. God will reveal those details over time."[2]

But what does the Word have to do with the Holy Spirit?

The Spirit empowers the Word of God.

When Andrew Murray went to the Moody Bible Institute in Chicago from South Africa in the summer of 1895, he gave a series of lectures to the students about how a Spirit-filled life was about more than the Spirit's empowerment for ministry. It was about the Spirit's empowerment for living. The students were so impressed with his series of lectures that with Murray's permission they turned his notes into a volume called *The Spiritual Life*, published originally in 1896. Murray wrote, "When the Spirit of God has filled a person, he can handle the sword of the Spirit, which is the Spirit of God. Without that filling it is not possible. This is the reason for so much preaching without fruit—because we use the sword of the Spirit without being filled with the Spirit."[3]

How then do we have a Spirit-filled life?

Charles Stanley said, "For years I believed it was my responsibility to wait on the Holy Spirit to fill me. At some point I guess I grew tired of waiting and tried to win Him or talk Him into filling me. Thus, all the praying and begging and fasting. But as Billy Graham stated so perfectly, 'This is the good news: We are no longer waiting for the Holy Spirit—He is waiting for us. We are no longer living in a time of promise, but a time of fulfillment.'"[4] The Holy Spirit has already come, just as Jesus promised. When we receive Jesus, the Holy Spirit lives inside of us. But there's an "even more" that a Christian can have with the Holy Spirit. "Holy Spirit, fill me with even more of your presence."

In Mezana's story, we will see a picture of what it means to wield the sword of the Spirit through the Spirit.

Mezana's Quest

As Mezana and Cara sat around the fire with Asriel, he suddenly leaned forward, his face aglow in the firelight. "I have a secret," he said.

"Tell us!" Cara begged.

"I have defeated the evil one."

Mezana reeled at this news. "The war is over then?"

"The evil one is cunning. He is defeated, but he still strives to kill, steal, and destroy my people."

Mezana nodded, thinking of the old lady from the market. "But if he's still attacking us, how can the war be over?"

"It's over because the evil one has lost his power," Asriel said as he reached for a long wooden box. He opened it, revealing a shiny sword. He carefully lifted it from the box's satin lining and held it up, letting the sword sparkle in the flickering light. Then Asriel leaned forward and blew his breath upon it. He looked up and said, "The power over the evil one is in my sword of the Spirit."

Mezana stared at the blade. It was beautiful, sharp, and shiny like gold. She blinked. There was something unusual about it. The sword was covered with—no, created from—words. In fact, it seemed to sing, "You are loved," as she stared at it.

Asriel picked up the sword by its ruby-encrusted handle and stood, towering above Mezana and Cara. Glowing in power and strength, Asriel swept the blade over their heads.

To Mezana's amazement, the blade sang words that poured over them like warm honey. "The Word has set you free!"

Mezana could feel the power of the sword's words, words that made her heart soar. "It's beautiful," she whispered. She looked to Asriel. "Is this sword what the evil one is after?"

Asriel laughed. "In part. But before I tell you the rest, I want to present this sword to you. To both of you."

For a moment, Mezana sat speechless. "To us? Aren't you afraid we'll lose it? Or worse yet, the evil one will steal it away?"

Asriel only smiled. "You mustn't worry. Of course, the evil one will try to steal it from you, but he will not be able to use its power because the sword also has a secret."

"What kind of secret?" Cara asked.

"I have breathed my life upon it. But be warned, if the evil one does manage to take it from you, even briefly, you could experience confusion, blindness, and even loss."

Mezana asked, "What should we do if that happens?"

"Only *remember* the sword. When you remember it, the sword will come back to you."

Cara, whose eyes were as big as saucers, asked, "Asriel, am I big enough to carry the sword?"

Asriel pulled the child into his lap and handed her an identical sword. "See, you are the perfect size."

Cara turned her sword over in her small hands. Asriel continued, "It will not harm you, but it will cut to the heart of the matter before you and also improve your understanding. You will be able to wield it mightily because your childlike heart will supply it with the power of simple faith."

Later that night Mezana and Cara carefully carried their swords home, amazed that such gifts could belong to them.

As Mezana tucked Cara into her bed, she saw that the girl had slipped her sword beneath her pillow. Mezana could only chuckle at the sweetness of it.

When Mezana herself got ready for bed, she contemplated where she should hide her sword so that if Beliah did break in he would not be able to find it. She first placed the sword beneath her bed, then she tucked it into the pantry. Finally, she thought of a place Beliah would never search. She swept her beautiful sword under the rug. With the deed done, she crawled into her bed and soon fell asleep.

In the wee hours of the morning, Mezana's worst fears came true. The door to her cottage burst open. By the time Mezana opened her eyes, Beliah was standing over her holding her own sword.

"Did you think you could hide this from me?" Beliah roared.

Mezana's mouth went dry, and her heart pounded in her ears. She sat up on one elbow confused, unable to react. In a flash, Cara was by her side. The child pointed her sword at the giant and simply said, "Asriel told us you are already defeated."

Suddenly words began to dance out of Cara's sword, filling the room with a blinding light.

Beliah screamed and held his eyes as he dropped Mezana's sword, which clattered to the floor. As Mezana remembered her sword, it flew into her hand, and she pointed it at the shrinking specter. "We have the victory," she cried. The room exploded with words of light, and Beliah continued to shrink until he was only a red-eyed mouse squeaking in rage.

Mezana and Cara stared at him, then grinned at each other. "He doesn't look so scary now," Cara said. Mezana shooed the creature out the door with the point of her blade. Beliah ran into the darkness, hissing and snarling though quite harmless.

Even after he left, the words from their swords continued to light the room and circle their heads. The word *life* wrote itself on the walls and doorjambs and scribbled itself across the floor. Mezana and Cara watched with joy. The sword of Asriel had brought victory, just as Asriel had said.

The Allegory Explained

It's a joy to see our allegory come alive with truths regarding the Word of God. I especially love the symbolism of our fictional Asriel breathing upon the sword made of the Word. Of course, this symbolism comes straight out of Paul's words in 2 Timothy 3:16, which says, "All Scripture is breathed out by God" (ESV).

The Word also serves as a weapon against the enemy, a weapon Jesus himself used when the Spirit led him into the desert to be tempted by the devil. What was at stake? If Jesus gave in to any of the temptations of the evil one, he would essentially be handing the devil complete domination over all humankind and would not become our Messiah. He would not set us free from sin and death. We would not be in God's kingdom but the devil's.

But for each temptation the devil presented to him, Jesus answered with the Word of God. The devil tempted Jesus, when he was hungry after a forty-day fast, to turn stones into bread. But Jesus said, "No! The Scriptures say, 'People do not live by bread alone, but by every word that comes from the mouth of God'" (Matt. 4:4 NLT).

When the devil tempted Jesus to jump off the temple, the devil quoted the Scripture passage that said, "He will order his angels to protect you. And they will hold you up with their hands so you won't even hurt your foot on a stone" (Matt. 4:6 NLT).

Jesus answered back with Scripture, saying, "The Scriptures also say, 'You must not test the Lord your God'" (Matt. 4:7 NLT).

Then finally when the devil tempted Jesus to bow to him, saying that he would give Jesus all the kingdoms of the earth, Jesus knew the truth of the matter. Satan was trying to capture the authority of Jesus, for if Jesus had given in to Satan's temptation, Jesus would have submitted to Satan's authority rather than God's authority. Jesus would have received a demotion to become a prince in the kingdom of darkness instead of the Savior of the world. So Jesus answered this temptation with the Word, saying, "Get out of here, Satan. . . . For the Scriptures say, 'You must worship the LORD your God and serve only him'" (Matt. 4:10 NLT).

Jesus triumphed over Satan's temptations through the power of the Word.

How precious is the Word! But if we want to brandish the Word like a sword against the wiles of the enemy, we must know it. And we know it by reading it, studying it, memorizing it, and praying it. Then we must allow the Holy Spirit within us to bring it to our remembrance whenever we face temptations, struggles, or hardships. The enemy still attacks, but he is powerless to stand up to the Word wielded under the anointing of God's Holy Spirit.

Paul Embraces His Calling to the Word

One of the churches Paul wrote to during his imprisonment in Rome was the house church at Colossae. Even though Paul had never visited Colossae, he was disturbed to learn that the church was mixing Christ's teachings with a philosophy called gnosticism. Gnosticism taught that the way to achieve salvation was through self by transcending the evil world by ignoring material and sexual desires.

It's true that Jesus calls us to turn from sin, but gnosticism ignored the truth that Jesus died on the cross for our sins, defeating sin and death through his resurrection.

When Paul wrote to the church at Colossae, he explained that he was a servant by the commission God gave him to present the Word of God in its fullness (Col. 1:25), saying, "God wanted his people throughout the world to know the glorious riches of this mystery—which is Christ living in you, giving you the hope of glory" (Col. 1:27 GW).

Paul showed the believers in Colossae the error of their ways so they could be set free from sin, move from death to life in Christ, and have the hope of glory. The Word does the same for us today.

The Armor

Hebrews 4:12 says, "God's Word is living and powerful. It is sharper than a sword that cuts both ways. It cuts straight into where the soul and spirit meet and it divides them. It cuts into the joints and bones. It tells what the heart is thinking about and what it wants to do" (NLV).

This description of God's Word resembles the Roman short sword, a blade about twenty inches in length that weighed two to three pounds. What made this blade so remarkable was that it had a double edge and could be used from any direction or angle. Soldiers used it to step inside an enemy's personal space and to stab without warning. When we learn how to battle with the sword of the Spirit, with its two edges of the Word and God's Holy Spirit, the enemy will flee before us.

Suiting Up

How do we ignite the Word with the Spirit? The Word is alive, but when we read it, quote it, believe it, and pray it, the life in the Word ignites with the power of the Holy Spirit, who dwells inside of us, creating a weapon we can use to defeat the enemy. But to be able to ignite the Word with the Holy Spirit, we must have the Spirit in our lives. In other words, it's all about relationship, as Charles Stanley explains: "Like every other aspect of the Christian life, the Spirit-filled life is a life of faith. I had been approaching it as if it were a formula; it is a relationship, a relationship with the Holy Spirit."[5]

You can always deepen your relationship with the Holy Spirit by welcoming him into your life, by asking for more of his presence and power. As the old saying goes, "You can have as much of God (and his Spirit) as you want."

Please don't close yourself off to the Spirit because you're afraid or because you don't understand him. Trust me, you need the Holy Spirit more than ever before. This Holy Spirit is the Spirit who was with Jesus and all the prophets. He is the one who gives us his fruit of "love, joy, peace, forbearance, kindness, goodness, faithfulness, gentleness and self-control" (Gal. 5:22–23). He is the one who empowers us, guides us, gives us strength and wisdom. He is the one who makes God's Word come alive and refreshes our hearts. He is our comforter. To push him away because we are afraid of him or what he might do is foolish. We must embrace him, welcome him, and seek even more of him in our lives. Trying to live the Christian life without him would be like "having a form of godliness but denying its power" (2 Tim. 3:5).

Let's not do that. Let's be brave and open to the indwelling of the Holy Spirit and his power. Then when we brandish the sword of the Spirit, it will empower us to be and to do all we can through Christ.

> *Dear Jesus,*
>
> *I thank you for all you did for me. You are the Word, you are the truth, you are the life. Show me how to stay in the Word so I can read it, quote it, believe it, remember it, and pray it. Ignite your Word with your Spirit and power so that my own spirit will be ignited with your Spirit. You are welcome in me, Holy Spirit. Please fill me with more of your Spirit. And more still. In Jesus's name, amen.*

ARMORED RESPONSE

Here's a chance to use the sword of the Spirit to break strongholds against you.

Captivity-Fighting Scripture

"I have given you the authority to trample snakes and scorpions and to destroy the enemy's power. Nothing will hurt you" (Luke 10:19 GW).

Declaration to Defeat Captivity

I declare that Jesus has given me the authority to trample on all manner of the enemy's weapons and strategies against me and to destroy the enemy's power. Nothing will hurt me.

Prayer for Victory over Captivity

Dear Lord,

I wield your sword of deliverance, praying Luke 10:19, igniting it with the power of your Holy Spirit. I pray that you would give me authority to trample the enemy's power, in whatever form it comes against me. Thank you that you will protect me and let nothing hurt me. Thank you that I am delivered from the power of the enemy and his schemes. In Jesus's name, amen.

9

Praying on All Occasions

Pray in the Spirit at all times and on every occasion. Stay alert and be persistent in your prayers for all believers everywhere.

Ephesians 6:18 NLT

A few weeks before my daughter was rushed to the ICU, the summer evening turned black as the tornado sirens blared. I looked out the window at the fast-moving sky and saw the stinger of a tornado rolling sideways over our house.

Were there more twisters to come?

I stood over the bed of my medically fragile daughter. Together we were about to face a day I'd hoped would never come. It wasn't supposed to. The word on the street was, "We're safe from tornados because the Colorado foothills protect us." But the trouble was that the fast-moving storm was blowing the wrong way, toward the mountains instead of east toward Kansas.

As the storm pressed itself against the mountains, the entire sky began to rotate. While quarter-size hail threatened to rain shards of glass from the skylight overhead, the air crackled with electricity.

How I longed to take my daughter into the basement, but her wheelchair wouldn't make the trip. Laura was too heavy to carry and too fragile to drag. So there we were, stuck in harm's way, with only a mattress and the name of Jesus to protect us.

Only the name of Jesus?

I stood and faced the blackness outside our window, commanding the tornado to go up in the name of Jesus.

The sky turned orange and the heavens roared like a freight train while I tucked Laura beneath her bed and continued to pelt heaven with my prayers. But the problem was the storm was stuck against the mountains and stayed there, rebuilding on itself for almost six hours. Just when I thought the terror would never stop, the storm ended with a boom of a nearby lightning strike.

Soon the news revealed that an EF3 tornado had passed only a mile away, destroying homes as it thundered toward the foothills. Later I learned that a second funnel cloud had passed right over my neighborhood before touching down a few miles away.

The next day I felt the urge to call a friend, a friend who wasn't quite ready to believe in God.

"Did you see the tornado?" I asked when she picked up the phone.

"Did I? I heard a noise outside and stepped onto my porch and looked up directly into the wall of the tornado just over my house. That's when I saw my neighbor's roof sail by."

"Did you get hit?"

"No, and the odd thing was the tornado jumped over my house before it exploded the rest of the neighborhood."

"Do you know what I was praying while that tornado was on the ground?" I asked.

"What?"

"Go up, tornado, go up in the name of Jesus!"

My friend sucked in her breath. "Well, I have to admit that was a really good prayer."

When you face a difficult situation, don't discount the name of Jesus, for the name of Jesus is more precious and more powerful than anything else you could rely on.[1]

Our Quest

The final weapon in Paul's famous armor passage is prayer. "Pray in the Spirit at all times and on every occasion. Stay alert and be persistent in your prayers for all believers everywhere" (Eph. 6:18 NLT).

Prayer helps us win our battles as we seek God's direction. It helps us accomplish our purposes in every area of our lives. Plus, it helps us stay connected with God and gives us a way to call for God's victory, support, relief, and comfort over situations, people, and causes.

Andrew Murray said:

> In its beginnings prayer is so simple that even a small child can pray, it is at the same time the highest and holiest work to which anyone can rise. It is fellowship with the unseen and most Holy One. The powers of the eternal world have been placed at its disposal. It is the channel of all blessing and

the secret of power and life. Through prayer God has given to everyone the right to take hold of Him and His strength.[2]

Ephesians 6:18 calls us to do the following when we pray:

- pray in the Spirit
- pray at all times
- pray on every occasion
- stay alert
- be persistent
- pray for others

Pray in the Spirit

How glad I am that Jesus promised us that upon completion of his earthly ministry he would not leave us as orphans but would send his Holy Spirit to be *in* us (John 14:16–17).

With the Spirit in us, we can pray in the Spirit whether we pray with understanding or not. It's like how my friend Dianne prayed as her body was rolling down the freeway at sixty-five miles an hour after her motorcycle crashed. When she prayed her one word prayer, "Jesus," she was expressing everything in her heart, though she didn't have the time to put all the words in her heart into a prayer. In other words, as Dianne rolled down the freeway, she became a sort of "holy roller" as she experienced a supernatural, Holy-Spirit-breathed prayer phenomenon. Paul explained this concept in Romans 8:26, "At the same time the Spirit also helps us in our weakness, because we don't know how to pray for what we need. But the Spirit intercedes along with our groans that cannot be expressed in words" (GW).

Pray at All Times

Paul called us to pray continually when he said, "Rejoice always, pray continually, give thanks in all circumstances; for this is God's will for you in Christ Jesus" (1 Thess. 5:16–18).

The Greek word for "pray continually" is *adialepitos*, meaning "without intermission, incessantly, without ceasing."[3]

Why does Paul call us to pray at all times? My friend Joy says, "Praying without ceasing means we are always in conversation with God. That's why I often put on praise music in my house, because when I am not talking to God, the music is in my ears, mind, and spirit and is talking to God for and with me."

Yes! I too find that worship music helps me pray without ceasing, for my heart sings the praise back to the Lord as I listen to the words of the songs.

Pray on Every Occasion

Of course, most of us would want to pray in the face of a tornado, but there are so many other reasons to go to prayer, including the needs of ourselves, others, and nations; sickness, disasters, and warfare; and praise, worship, and thanksgiving.

In other words, no matter the occasion, we should pray. We should pray upon rising, upon resting, upon dining, upon commuting to work, upon working, at church, outside of church, for our relationships, when tempted, at play, at rest. There is no occasion that doesn't merit prayer, including when we are doing the very thing we know we shouldn't do. "Forgive me and help me turn from this behavior" would be a good prayer to pray on such an occasion.

Stay Alert

Okay, I admit it. A few days ago I noticed spider webs above my back door and did nothing. I meant to, but I forgot about them. That is, until I decided to let my dog out one last time before retiring for the evening. I snapped on the porch light and stepped outside. In that moment, unbeknownst to me, a large spider landed on my head.

That's when I heard a loud flap and looked up just in time to see a bat leap out of a cubbyhole in the portico above my head and dive directly at me. As I raised my arm for protection, I felt the velvety softness of the bat's body. I was laughing, screaming, falling backward, trying to pull the dog inside, and trying to shut the door so the bat wouldn't get into the house.

My adult son came running. "What happened?"

I couldn't speak because I was still screaming and laughing. My son, Jim, responded to my hysterics by saying, "There's a large spider on your head."

I finally found my words. "There is not."

"I'm not kidding."

I swatted at my head and watched as the spider flew through the air to land on my son, a young man who is not too fond of these creatures. I said, "It's not on my head anymore. The spider is on you!"

"It is not," my son said.

Afraid of how he might react if he actually saw that large spider on his chest, I swatted at the spider until I knocked it off.

Finally, I said, "It *was* on you."

"So I gathered," he replied.

That's when I realized I had tiny welts on my arm from where I'd come in contact with the bat.

When I showed the welts to Jim, he said, "Mom, no arguments. I'm taking you to the ER! That bat could have rabies, and getting rabies is worse than getting Ebola!"

After waiting in the ER for hours, I finally had a chance to tell the doctor and nurse what happened. They looked confused. "Have you been drinking?" the nurse asked.

"I don't drink."

"What have you ingested this evening?"

"Water, roasted chicken, and veggies," I said.

"Any mushrooms with that?"

"Nope."

The doctor followed up, "This is a highly unusual story. Are you on drugs?"

"I don't take drugs."

"But you take pharmaceuticals. What are you on?"

"I don't take pharmaceuticals, unless you want to count Tylenol."

He looked skeptical, so I ventured, "I took two before I came in. I guess I get headaches from bat attacks. Probably the stress, right?"

The doctor stared at me without blinking. This was a middle-of-the-night ER doctor who usually dealt with a lot of stoned and intoxicated folks. I guess he didn't get a sober, bat storyteller all that often. So in a way, I understood his confusion.

It was only after my son corroborated what must have seemed like a tall tale that the doctor ordered a series of rabies shots.

I have a confession. I do not believe the bat would have swooped down at me like that if I had not been wearing a spider. All of these theatrics could have been avoided if I had taken a broom to the cobwebs above my back door, something I did the very next day. I also had my husband stuff steel wool in the cubbyhole where the bat had been hiding.

Perhaps you are like me. You see the danger, but you don't do anything about it. Or maybe the enemy sneaks in a surprise attack, just like a bat swooping toward your head.

So what is the moral of the story?

Stay alert! When you see or contemplate sin, avoid it. Step away. Remove the temptation. Turn another direction. Call out to Jesus in prayer. Otherwise, your sin could attract an attack from the enemy.

Be Persistent

Have you ever heard of the acronym PUSH, Pray Until Something Happens? That's actually what Jesus is saying in Matthew 7:7–8: "Keep on asking, and you will receive what you ask for. Keep on seeking, and you will find. Keep on knocking, and the door will be opened to you. For everyone who asks, receives. Everyone who seeks, finds. And to everyone who knocks, the door will be opened" (NLT).

It's easy to get discouraged and give up on prayer, but instead we should think about the story Jesus told about the persistent widow who continued to plead for justice from an unrighteous judge. Jesus said, "The judge ignored her for a while, but finally he said to himself, 'I don't fear God or care about people, but this woman is driving me crazy. I'm going to see that she gets justice, because she is wearing me out with her constant requests!'" (Luke 18:4–5 NLT).

Jesus finished his parable with this teaching:

Learn a lesson from this unjust judge. Even he rendered a just decision in the end. So don't you think God will surely give justice to his chosen people who cry out to him day and night? Will he keep putting them off? I tell you, he will grant justice to them quickly! But when the Son of Man returns, how many will he find on the earth who have faith? (Luke 18:6–8 NLT)

When we pray persistently, we are not nagging God because we are afraid he's unjust. We persistently pray because God is persistently faithful.

So keep on praying, and keep your eyes open for the victory, which will appear. Victory, though, could appear in a way you wouldn't expect. Be open to God's answers even when they first appear disguised as disappointments. Wait and watch God turn your disappointments into divine purpose.

Pray for Others

If we want to join in the work of Jesus, we should pray for others. As Hebrews 7:24–25 explains, "But because Jesus lives forever, he has a permanent priesthood. Therefore he is able to save completely those who come to God through him, because he always lives to intercede for them."

Cheri Fuller says, "I've found one of the most remarkable aspects of prayer: that when we pray for others, we are joining the Savior in his full-time eternal vocation—making intercession for the saints."[4] She goes on to say, "It is a profound mystery that when we pray, we are joining the Son who sits on the throne next to the Father in highest heaven. It is his life, his Spirit within us that is praying as we live and move and have our being with him."[5]

When we pray for others, we are fulfilling one of our purposes. We are joining Jesus in the work he has called us to do.

Mezana's Quest

One evening Asriel dropped by Mezana and Cara's cottage. The pair was overjoyed to see him. Cara grabbed his hand and tugged him through the door and invited him to sit down at their table. As Mezana poured him a cool drink of water, Asriel motioned for her to sit beside him. "I have something important to discuss with you."

As Mezana pulled up a chair, she asked, "What is it, dear Asriel?"

"I am going away," he told them.

"No!" Cara said, her eyes filling with tears. Asriel reached for the child and pulled her into his lap as she asked, "Please, can we come with you?"

Asriel shook his head. "You may not go where I am going, but know that I will be here with you in spirit."

Mezana was overcome with tears, and Asriel lifted her chin with a touch of his hand. "When have you called to me that I haven't answered?" he asked her.

"You were always there when I needed you."

"And that will not change," Asriel promised her.

"But I don't understand."

"You will," Asriel said, "for tonight I have come to tell you my good-byes."

Long hours after Asriel had left, Mezana and Cara still wept together. "How could he go?" Cara asked. "Doesn't he understand how much we love and need him?"

Mezana couldn't answer. She had no words to explain.

Some days later Mezana was kneading dough when a knock sounded at the door. She wiped her hands on her apron and ran to answer.

There before her stood a weasely man. He said, "Name's Theib and I own this house. I've come to collect my rent."

Mezana was surprised. "I wasn't aware I had a landlord."

"Do you think you can live here for free?"

"Well, I . . ."

Theib peered into the room at Cara, then turned back to Mezana.

"You owe me a thousand shekels, my dear."

Mezana gasped. "I can't pay you that!"

An evil grin spread over Theib's thin lips. "That's a pity, but I do take other things in trade." He pointed to the girl. "That one would fetch a fine price at the slave market."

"She's not for sale!" Mezana blurted.

"That leaves you." Theib grabbed Mezana's arm, his bony fingers fixed in a tight grip. "And your debt is past due."

Theib dragged Mezana from her home. "You were born to be sold in the slave market," he told her. "It's your destiny."

"Call out to Asriel," Cara cried, chasing after them.

Theib sneered. "Asriel? Rumor is he's left for parts unknown."

"Asriel!" Mezana whispered, her voice hoarse with fear.

Theib's laughter covered her frail call. But Cara's voice joined Mezana's cry, and together they shouted, "Asriel! We need you."

Suddenly, Asriel, in a flash of blinding light, stood before them. "What do you think you are doing, Theib?" he demanded.

Theib pulled his hand away from Mezana's arm. "We were only walking together, Asriel, nothing more."

Cara blurted, "He was dragging Mezana to the slave market!"

Mezana explained, "Theib says I owe him a thousand shekels to pay my rent."

"Rent?" Asriel stared at Theib with narrow eyes. "As you know, Theib, I own this cottage, not you. No rent is due."

Theib backed away. "Just a misunderstanding, Asriel. No harm done," he said as he turned and bolted down the road.

Cara and Mezana stared at Asriel. "I thought you had left us," Mezana said.

Asriel answered, "I am still with you in spirit. Call upon me whenever you can. It will keep us close. I am coming back soon."

With those words he was gone, leaving the sweetness of his spirit to linger in their hearts.

The Allegory Explained

In this part of our story, we see the parallel of Jesus telling his disciples he must leave them before the Comforter comes. The disciples were grieved at the news and didn't yet understand how dear the Holy Spirit would become to them.

Today we have the presence of the Holy Spirit in our lives. He is the One who gives us power to pray and to call upon the name of Jesus. Meanwhile, the thief is still in the business of lying, stealing, and destroying. But the Holy Spirit is in the business of guiding our prayers, illuminating the truth, setting us free, and indwelling us. Someday we will be united with

Jesus after our final breath here on earth. But for now, we have Jesus's name, his salvation, and his Spirit. We are truly blessed.

Paul Prays for Publius's Father

Something interesting happened after Paul was shipwrecked on the island of Malta. The leader of the island, a man named Publius, invited Paul into his home. Let's see what Acts 28:8–9 says happened next: "The father of Publius was sick with a stomach sickness. Paul went to see him. He prayed and laid his hands on him and the man was healed. Because of this, other people of the island who were sick came to Paul and were healed" (NLV).

In other words, a revival resulted because of Paul's answered prayer for Publius's sick father. I'm guessing this was at least part of the reason God allowed Paul to be shipwrecked on this island on his way to Rome. For the revival to come, however, Paul had to be willing to pray for a sick man. And God had to be willing to heal not only Publius's father but also the sick islanders who also came for prayer.

Healing prayer is one of the ways God calls unbelievers to himself. So take a lesson from Paul and pray on all occasions, even when shipwrecked, even for the sick, even for the souls of your friends and family, then leave the results to God. That's true faith. Don't be afraid to pray persistently as God leads.

The Armor

When you think about it, this weapon of prayer is actually made from the words on our lips and in our hearts. Our intercessions for others as well as ourselves are battle cries. Our battle cries, or our prayers of faith, may be the weapon that causes the devil to tremble the most.

I've collected some famous prayers that were used as battle cries to illustrate how the best of the best prayed for miracles. We'll start this recital with a revisit of David rushing at Goliath with his slingshot. Young David shouted, "I come to you in the name of the Lord of All, the God of the armies of Israel, Whom you have stood against" (1 Sam. 17:45 NLV). David let a single stone fly and felled the giant.

Then there was the battle cry of praise orchestrated through King Jehoshaphat's choir as it led the army of Israel to a battle. The choir sang, "Give thanks to the LORD; his faithful love endures forever" (2 Chron. 20:21 NLT). The battle was fought and the enemy defeated even before the choir and soldiers arrived on the battlefield.

And we can't forget the battle cry of Elijah as he faced off against the prophets of Baal. "O Lord, God of Abraham, Isaac and Israel, let it be known today that You are God in Israel. Let it be known that I am Your servant, and have done all these things at Your word" (1 Kings 18:36 NLV). God rained fire on Elijah's sacrifice, and the people of Israel knew Jehovah was the true God, not Baal, and Baal worship was defeated in the land.

Then there is the most important battle cry of all, the battle cry that opened the gates of hell, defeating both sin and death. Our Lord and Savior Jesus cried out on the cross, "It is finished" (John 19:30). When we trust in Jesus, our sins are forgiven and God's Holy Spirit comes to dwell in our lives.

Finally, there is the prayer we can all pray to defeat the enemy and overturn his works: "In the name of Jesus, I declare the victory in this situation by the power of the blood of Jesus!" The victory is won!

These are all great prayer examples to remember whenever we are in the heat of a battle.

Suiting Up

One of my favorite things about the weapon of prayer is that I am not the one responsible for answering my prayers. That is fully up to God. Yet I am responsible for praying, trusting that God hears, and trusting that he is moving. Prayer is a weapon I can use against the enemy with complete trust in God, for I am calling out to God not only in the name of Jesus but also in Jesus, with Jesus, through Jesus, to Jesus, and in agreement with Jesus. How wonderful is that? Let's try it now.

> *Dear Lord,*
>
> *I am calling out to you in the name of Jesus, in Jesus, with Jesus, through Jesus, to Jesus, and in agreement with Jesus. I am calling out to you, saying that my problem of _____ is no match for the God of the universe. The God I praise and worship is good, and his love endures forever.*
>
> *Lord, let it be known that I am your servant and that I am following you and your will. Jesus won the battle on the cross. All is finished in and through him. So now I declare victory over _____ in the name of Jesus, by the power of the blood of Jesus! In Jesus's name, amen.*

ARMORED RESPONSE

Here's a chance to use the weapon of prayer to break through your troubles.

Trouble-Fighting Scripture

"He will call upon Me, and I will answer him. I will be with him in trouble. I will take him out of trouble and honor him" (Ps. 91:15 NLV).

Declaration to Defeat Trouble

I declare that when I call upon the Lord, I have faith that he will answer me, that he will be with me in times of trouble. The Lord will take me out of trouble and set me in a place to reflect his love and glory.

Prayer for Victory over Trouble

Dear Lord,

I wield your weapon of prayer, praying Psalm 91:15, igniting it with the power of the Word and your Holy Spirit. I pray that you will answer me when I call upon you. You will be with me in any trouble, and you will get me out of my trouble and honor me with your love and provision. In Jesus's name, amen.

10

Defeating the Strongman

Put on all of God's armor so that you will be able to stand firm against all strategies of the devil. For we are not fighting against flesh-and-blood enemies, but against evil rulers and authorities of the unseen world, against mighty powers in this dark world, and against evil spirits in the heavenly places.

Ephesians 6:11–12 NLT

When Rose was a sweet sixteen-year-old girl, she joined a club for teen girls that was supposed to be Christian in nature. At least that's what Rose's friends told her. Though when Rose pressed for more information about the group, her friends' answers were vague and mysterious. The next thing Rose knew she was dressed in a white gown as she partook in an ancient ceremony worshiping Greek gods and declaring violent oaths as to what would happen if she ever told the group's secrets.

Rose, who loved Jesus with all her heart, was horrified. Still, she went along with the ceremony, telling herself that she and her friends were only playacting and that no one could possibly mean the horrible things they were saying. But by the end of the meeting, Rose had changed her mind about the innocence of what the group was up to. She was convinced she had joined some sort of cult.

When her mother came to pick her up that night, Rose slid into the car and with many tears told her mother she would never return to this gathering, and she didn't.

In her forties, Rose thought this incident was well behind her. But still, she wondered why, through the years, the enemy seemed to have an open door into her life, a life plagued by heartache and tragedy.

Then Rose met a group of believers who explained that when she'd participated in the oaths and declarations to the Greek gods, she had opened the door to the enemy and that door was still open.

Rose said, "Now I finally understood why I'd experienced little victory in my life against my battle with the enemy. It's hard to have victory in a battle when the door to your bunker is wide open."

So what did Rose do? How did she close the door?

Rose's believing friends helped her break the oaths and curses she'd made with the occult. They did so by helping Rose call upon the power and authority of the name and the blood of Jesus. "Forgive me for worshiping other gods. I renounce the oaths and proclamations I made to them. I declare this in the power of the name and the blood of Jesus. I break the curses off of me in the power of the name and the blood of Jesus."[1] This prayer is what finally helped shore up

Rose's defense against the enemy. Rose later said, "Do I ever understand Eve. Eve was deceived in the Garden of Eden by the lies of a serpent. I was deceived by the lies of my friends. I had to go to Jesus and confess my sin of opening the door to a false god and ask Jesus for his forgiveness and for his help to break the curses. The good news is Jesus forgave me and closed the door to the strongman. The enemy is defeated!"

You can bet my friend is careful to wear God's armor. And the bonus? She now experiences victory and protection in Christ instead of defeat.[2]

Mark Bubeck stated, "Satan's kingdom is engaged in a relentless effort to destroy Christians and their effective fulfillment of the will of God."[3] It's true. The enemy attacks us most in the areas of our purpose. For Rose, the enemy tried to destroy God's purpose for her as a mother by destroying the lives of her kids. Rose is now standing up to the strongman's attempts to harm her children by using the weapons of our warfare, and she is winning the battle.

What does this story mean to those of us who have never worshiped false gods? Unfortunately, there are many other doors that we can willfully or inadvertently open to the enemy, giving him legal right to lie, steal, kill, and destroy. So walk through the house of your life and test the doors to see if they are locked tight against things like lies, willful choices, pornography, illicit sexual encounters, gossip, unforgiveness, bitterness, self-pity, jealousy, drugs, dark media and the occult.

What do you do if you realize you've never shut a door to a sin or a traumatic past? You shut it.

How? You shut it when you go to Jesus, confess and turn from your sin or past, and ask Jesus to help you secure the door against the enemy. He will forgive you and help you close any door you have left open!

Here's a great prayer you can pray against the mistakes and traumas of your past as well as mistakes that could trip you in the present or future:

Dear Lord,

Thank you that your salvation and forgiveness apply to me regardless of my past. I repent of any sin or any part I may have played in a past experience. If I was an innocent victim, I still ask for your grace to cover me. I shut the door to this wrong or past experience in the power and authority of the name and the blood of Jesus. As the ancient Israelites sprinkled the blood of a lamb on their doorpost to ward off the angel of death, I sprinkle the blood of Jesus, the true sacrificial lamb, on the doorpost of my life and declare that I'm free from the power of sin and death. I choose to turn from my sin and past in and with and through your power. I break all evil soul ties or connections with my past or past incidents. I declare that I accept the life Jesus so freely offers me. With your help, give me the power to shut the door to any legal rights of torment, evil soul ties, lies, oaths, curses, death, theft, and destruction that the enemy may have had over my life. I shut the door in your power, in you, through you, in agreement with you, and in the power of the name and the blood of Jesus.

This is a powerful prayer! Not long ago I was praying with a friend who told me the enemy sometimes plagued her like dark crows sitting on a fence. I asked her, "Do you know what to say to a crow?"

She shook her head. "What?"

"Shoo!"

It really is that simple. When the dark crows of the enemy land on your fence—crows of sin, lies, harassment, and temptation—you have the right to say, "Shoo in the power and authority of the name and the blood of Jesus."

Our Quest

If you really want to keep the crows out of your life, wear the armor of God. It is more powerful than any scarecrow when it comes to protecting you from the ravaging effects of sin and the enemy's attacks. As Ephesians 6 states, "Put on all of God's armor so that you will be able to stand firm against all strategies of the devil. For we are not fighting against flesh-and-blood enemies, but against evil rulers and authorities of the unseen world, against mighty powers in this dark world, and against evil spirits in the heavenly places" (vv. 11–12 NLT). The purpose of the armor is to help us stand up to the enemy and his strategies so we can move forward in our God-given purposes.

If you find, however, that you've followed the crows of compromise into sin, close the door to that sin by confessing it and turning from it. Then you can have the freedom to pray as did a repentant King David after his affair with Bathsheba: "But you, O Lord, are a shield around me; you are my glory, the one who holds my head high" (Ps. 3:3 NLT).

Our God is faithful and offers us forgiveness as well as his own shield to surround us. Lawrence Richards explains, "He has bestowed glory on you by choosing you, blessing you and adopting you as His own child. He will never forsake you. In His faithfulness, He will extinguish every arrow hurled by the evil one. So lift high the shield of God's faithfulness. And remember that you are safe."[4]

Mezana's Quest

Mezana carefully checked the door of her cottage to make sure it was locked before she slipped into bed. In the silence of her room, Mezana was so overcome by sadness that she turned her face to her pillow and wept. It had been such a long time since she had seen Asriel, and her heart literally ached for his return. He had promised her he'd come back, but weeks had turned to months, and she was losing heart. Where was he? Did he still live? Did he still care about her?

True, the sweetness of his spirit lingered, especially when she whispered his name. But she was lonely and wanted to see him face-to-face. Her real question, she realized, was this: Was she really lonely or simply alone?

Sure, Asriel had rescued her from the slave camp, he had redeemed her with his good name, and he had given her many weapons to keep the evil one at bay. He had promised her the sweetness of his spirit. But still, she missed him. Finally, in her loneliness, she whispered into the darkness, "I'd rather be dead than feel the heartache of feeling so alone."

As Mezana drifted to sleep, she did not hear the click of the bolt in her back door. She did not see the shadow move toward her bed. She did not see the strongman looming over her until she felt his grip.

"You are to come with me," he told her.

Mezana stared up at the giant, her heart pounding. He was the most menacing figure she'd ever seen, at least ten feet tall with bulging muscles. His eyes were dead, and his sneer was made of pure hate.

Mezana could barely breathe, but she managed to whimper, "You have no right to take me."

The strongman jeered, "I do. I have the legal right to torment you."

She sat up. "But I belong to Asriel."

"That may be true, but I'm here by your invitation."

Mezana protested. "I would *never* invite you."

The strongman grabbed Mezana's arm and pulled her from her bed before throwing her hard against the wall. Mezana fell, her head slamming into the floor.

"But you did," the strongman said as he towered over her. "I'm here to give death to your hopes and dreams and even worse."

Awakened by the crash, Cara ran into the room holding her sword. "Stop!" she cried as she pointed it at the strongman. He only laughed but with a hollowness that echoed on the walls.

The strongman began to drag Mezana toward the door.

"Stop! In the name of Asriel!" Cara shouted again.

By now Mezana was weeping so bitterly that she could barely speak except to say, "This must be Asriel's will for me, Cara, to be tormented by the strongman."

"No!" Cara screamed. "How could you believe such a lie?"

Cara rushed to Mezana and tossed her the belt of truth. "Here!"

As Mezana tied truth around her waist, she looked up at the strongman. Though her head pounded from her fall, her mind cleared. "Cara is right. I do not belong to you."

"No? But you made an agreement with death when you made your vow, 'I'd rather be dead.' I've come to torment you and to drag you to death himself. He is waiting for you in the shadows."

"Asriel told me he came so I might have life," Mezana countered as she stood and grabbed her golden cap and placed it on her head. She slipped into her sandals of peace and felt a new strength surge through her. She had the power to take a step toward the strongman and said, "I renounce any words I made in agreement with you or with death. I declare life over me and announce that I belong to Asriel!"

The strongman rubbed his cheek as if he'd been slapped by a powerful hand and then scowled. "You may have stopped my plans for you this night, but I will be waiting for your careless words or deeds to trip you. Then I will return to torment you."

"And if you return, it is my right to repent of my words and deeds and to send you away in the name of Asriel," Mezana said, picking up her shield. She pointed her sword at the strongman. "It's time for you to go."

The strongman stumbled through the door and into the dark and growled, "I will be waiting."

Mezana and Cara hurried to bolt the door behind him.

Mezana bent down and gave the girl a squeeze. "I am so sorry. I didn't know my own words had the power to open the door to the strongman," she said.

"But you know now," Cara said, hugging her back.

"I made a careless mistake. Though I belong to Asriel, I must do my part to keep the door to my house bolted shut to our enemy."

The Allegory Explained

In this part of our story, we see that Mezana carelessly and unwittingly made a covenant with death through her words, unlocking the door to the strongman's harassment and evil schemes. Perhaps this is another reason we should be "careful little mouth what you say," as the children sing in Sunday school. Our words have power to make agreement with the enemy over ourselves as well as over the lives of others. So as we slip into our armor, we must be careful to put a guard on our mouths, for the tongue is a sword for both good and evil. James 3:5–10 says:

> A large forest can be set on fire by a little flame. The tongue is that kind of flame. It is a world of evil among the parts of our bodies, and it completely contaminates our bodies. The tongue sets our lives on fire, and is itself set on fire from hell. People have tamed all kinds of animals, birds, reptiles, and sea creatures. Yet, no one can tame the tongue. It is an uncontrollable evil filled with deadly poison.
>
> With our tongues we praise our Lord and Father. Yet, with the same tongues we curse people, who were created in God's likeness. Praise and curses come from the same mouth. My brothers and sisters, this should not happen! (GW)

Agreed. So let's be careful.

Along with evil words, our misdeeds can have ugly consequences. For example, if I shove a friend, even apologizing as my friend falls to the ground, my friend may end up hurt because of my actions. And that hurt could have ramifications for me, especially if I have to pay my friend's ambulance bill or, worse yet, have to make bail on an assault charge.

In other words, disobedient deeds can set things in motion that open the door to regret. When this happens, take your disobedience to the Lord, confess it, and ask the Lord for his grace. His grace may not take away every consequence of the hurt your deeds may have caused, but his grace will help you endure and heal and may even promote you to new purposes in ministry.

Paul Is Hindered by Satan

I know many people who do not believe Satan hinders believers. I have often shared examples of my own hindrances with friends, and they've said, "That's just a coincidence. Just because you happened to find an illustration of Satanists sacrificing a baby—that mysteriously appeared in your online newsletter—doesn't mean you are experiencing spiritual warfare. That kind of warfare just doesn't happen!"

What?

What if I told you this "silly" example is not so silly. It actually happened to me last week. That horrendous illustration mysteriously appeared in the first issue of my online newsletter that went out to readers on my Twitter feed.

Yikes!

I had to send out an apology letter. "Please know I did not put that illustration in the newsletter that was sent out. Please forgive me if you received it! I am taking measures to correct the situation so this never happens again."

Spiritual warfare measures, that is.

Okay, I'll agree with you that my illustration example is strange, and maybe you don't even believe it because nothing *that* strange has ever happened to you. I can appreciate that, but if you are in any sort of ministry connected to event planning, you might remember a time when everything that could go wrong did go wrong. Your website went down. Your phone and fax went out. Your flyers were printed with incorrect information. Your volunteers had a crisis and left you in the lurch. Your own family had a crisis. The chairs you needed didn't arrive. Etcetera, etcetera, etcetera. In other words, it was like the enemy was trying to hinder you. Right?

Or maybe you're a regular Joe trying to follow Christ, and you felt impressed to tell someone you know about Jesus, but something hindered your heart. Maybe it was a whisper like, "Do it later." But somehow later never came. Believe it or not, this too was a hindrance from Satan.

The apostle Paul recorded that he experienced hindrances from Satan in his ministry. For example, Paul told the church at Thessalonica, "Therefore we wanted to come to you—even I, Paul, time and again—but Satan hindered us" (1 Thess. 2:18 NKJV).

C. H. Spurgeon said in a sermon he delivered in 1865, "It has been Satan's practice of old to hinder, wherever he could, the work of God. 'Satan hindered us,' is the testimony which all the saints in heaven will bear against the arch enemy. This is the witness of all who have written a holy line on the historic page, or carved a consecrated name on the rock of immortality—'Satan hindered us.'"[5]

To be clear, Satan will try to hinder us most in our areas of purpose. In fact, Spurgeon said:

> How often, too, has Satan hindered us when we have entered into the work! In fact, beloved, we never ought to expect a success unless we hear the devil making a noise. I have taken it as a certain sign that I am doing little good when the devil is quiet. It is generally a sign that Christ's kingdom is coming when men begin to lie against you, and slander you, and the world is in an uproar, casting out your name as evil. Oh, those blessed tempests![6]

I've noted too that the bigger the hindrance, the bigger the victory, whether God removes the hindrance, helps me push through the hindrance, or turns the hindrance into a blessing. Even Paul himself understood this, as he wrote in Romans 8:28, "And we know that God causes everything to work together for the good of those who love God and are called according to his purpose for them" (NLT).

But still, who wants to deal with hindrances? It's just not good PR for the church to say, "If you follow Jesus, you can expect a hindrance or two along the way."

So then why follow Jesus and set yourself up like that?

Because he first loved us. Because he set us free from sin and death. Because he called to us, "Come, follow me!" (Luke 18:22 NLT). If for no other reason, follow Jesus because eternity without him is hell.

So never mind that the enemy hinders us or seems to have an occasional victory against us, because the good news is we win! In fact, we have already won!

Peter added to this conversation when he said:

Dear friends, don't be surprised at the fiery trials you are going through, as if something strange were happening to you. Instead, be very glad—for these trials make you partners with Christ in his suffering, so that you will have the wonderful joy of seeing his glory when it is revealed to all the world. If you are insulted because you bear the name of Christ, you will be blessed, for the glorious Spirit of God rests upon you. (1 Pet. 4:12–14 NLT)

Then in verse 19, Peter says, "So if you are suffering in a manner that pleases God, keep on doing what is right, and trust your lives to the God who created you, for he will never fail you" (NLT).

He will never fail us, even in the face of trials and hindrances.

Dear Lord,

Forgive me for having open doors. Show me when and where they exist, and give me the power and strength to close them.

I declare your life over me and break any vow of death I may have made over myself or others. In addition, I break all agreements I may have made with the strongman through my own thoughts or words or actions or sins. I declare life over me, over my hopes and dreams as well as the purposes you have for me.

I declare that in you, despite any trials or hindrances, I have the victory. You will never fail.

To defeat the enemy during a hindrance, I will continue to praise you, for when I praise you, the enemy's hindrances disappear. So I praise you now! You are wonderful, glorious, and my Redeemer. In the face of every trial, I will say, "Thank you, Lord," for everything. I tell the enemy to leave my situation or problem in the power and authority of the name of Jesus because I am dedicating the victory to God. In Jesus's name, amen.

ARMORED RESPONSE

If you are ready to see the enemy flee before you, check out this powerful promise of victory.

Spiritual Warfare–Fighting Scripture

"So humble yourselves before God. Resist the devil, and he will flee from you" (James 4:7 NLT).

Declaration to Defeat Spiritual Warfare

I declare that I humble myself before the Lord, and further declare that I will praise him, turn from sin, and shut all open doors so I can resist the devil and his schemes so he will flee from me.

Prayer for Victory over Spiritual Warfare

Dear Lord,

Thank you that many doors to the enemy stay closed unless I open them. Therefore, I humble myself before you and ask that you give me wisdom to serve you by not opening any doors to the strongman. If doors are open, show me where they are and help me to close them. Help me to resist the enemy's schemes and temptations to say or do that which would open doors and allow him into my life and situations. That way, when I call upon your name, the enemy will flee from me. In Jesus's name, amen.

11

Breakthrough to Your Purpose

So I run straight to the goal with purpose in every step. I fight to win.

1 Corinthians 9:26 TLB

Recently, a couple of hours after I put my favorite watch around my wrist, I noticed it had stopped. A couple of days later my second and then my third watch died, and I was left watchless. I joked to a friend, "I hope this isn't some sort of sign, like the end of time."

Bonnie laughed. "It's a sign that you should buy some batteries so your watches can have new life," she said.

A few days later I watched a clerk at a jewelry counter replace the batteries in my watches and was delighted to see each of my timepieces begin to tick away.

In many ways, watching the new batteries bring a fresh charge to my old watches was a picture of breakthrough.

Though the watches looked dead, all they needed was new life from a fresh battery.

The same can be said of us. When we've been stopped from fulfilling our purposes, we can call on the Lord of breakthrough. He recharges us as he defeats the lies, the harassments, and the hindrances of the enemy so we can redeem the time God has given us.

Our Quest

We should use our time to fulfill the purposes God has called us to. Paul said, "So I run straight to the goal with purpose in every step. I fight to win" (1 Cor. 9:26 TLB). Charles Stanley reminds us, "We have so little time, and yet from God's perspective we have just the right amount of time to do what he has ordained for us to do."[1]

That's comforting to know. All we have to do is follow God. As Max Lucado says, "God leads us. God will do the right thing at the right time. And what a difference that makes."[2] God is our guide through it all. Lucado describes the process by saying, "God isn't behind me yelling, 'Go!' He is ahead of me bidding, 'Come!' He is in front, clearing the path, cutting the brush, showing the way. Just before the curve he says, 'Turn here.' Prior to the rise, he motions, 'Step up here.' Standing next to the rocks he warns, 'Watch your step here.'"[3] This means we do not even have to figure out the solutions to our struggles. Lucado reminds us, "He leads us. He tells us what we need to know when we need to know it."[4]

But there's one thing we all need to realize. God has given each of us gifts to use on our journey. These gifts are like clues as to what our purposes are. It's time to understand and use your gifts so you can achieve your purpose. As Paul explained in Romans 12:

> Just as there are many parts to our bodies, so it is with Christ's body. We are all parts of it, and it takes every one of us to make it complete, for we each have different work to do. So we belong to each other, and each needs all the others.
>
> God has given each of us the ability to do certain things well. So if God has given you the ability to prophesy, then prophesy whenever you can—as often as your faith is strong enough to receive a message from God. If your gift is that of serving others, serve them well. If you are a teacher, do a good job of teaching. If you are a preacher, see to it that your sermons are strong and helpful. If God has given you money, be generous in helping others with it. If God has given you administrative ability and put you in charge of the work of others, take the responsibility seriously. Those who offer comfort to the sorrowing should do so with Christian cheer. (vv. 4–8 TLB)

Mezana's Quest

Mezana was asleep until she heard a light tapping on the front door of her cottage. She swung her feet over her bed and tiptoed through the dark house. Had the strongman returned?

"Who's there?" she whispered as Cara appeared by her side.

A woman's voice answered from the other side of the door, "Asriel sent us."

"Asriel!" Cara cried. Before Mezana could stop the child, she unbolted the door and swung it open.

Three strangers slipped inside, and a tall man dressed in armor said, "My name is Seth. I take it you are Mezana and Cara?"

One of the women, a soft-faced grandmother, took off her helmet, revealing her gray curls, and confided, "I'm Mercy, and this is Faith."

A blonde woman grasped Mezana's hand and grinned.

Seth continued, "Sorry for our intrusion at this hour, but we are here on an urgent matter."

"What matter do you mean?" Mezana asked, putting her arm around Cara.

Seth said, "It seems that the evil one has taken a group of orphans hostage in the dark woods. Asriel has called upon us to rescue them."

"Oh, the poor dears!" Mercy cried.

"The dark woods? We'll never survive such a trip, not before sunrise," Mezana stammered.

"The hour matters not," Seth explained. "What matters is that we follow the purposes Asriel has set for us."

Faith agreed and turned to Mezana and Cara. "Girls, get your armor on because we've got some kids to rescue."

Cara and Mezana quickly slipped into their armor and grabbed their swords as Mezana declared, "If Asriel called me to this task, I will go."

"There's one more thing," Seth explained as he pulled a little book out of his knapsack. "Asriel asked us to go in the power of the Word!"

"A book! May I carry it?" Cara asked.

"You can read?" Seth asked.

164

Cara nodded. "Mezana taught me," she said beaming.

Soon the group slipped into the night and trudged stealthily down a winding trail that led them up a rocky hillside. When they arrived at the edge of the dark woods, they could hear whispers of anguish in the evening's breeze.

"How will we find our way in this darkness?" Mezana whispered as they entered the shadows and brambles. "I can't see the way."

"The Word!" Cara said, opening the book. She read, "Your word is a lamp for my feet and a light for my path" (Ps. 119:105 GW).

A glow radiated from the open pages of the book, emitting just enough light to help the band move forward one step at a time.

Suddenly, they heard the cries of the orphans. Mercy was almost blinded with compassion. "Hurry! We must help them!" she whispered, wiping her eyes.

The band crept closer to the evil one's camp, closer than Mezana would have dared if Faith hadn't encouraged her. In the dancing firelight, she and her band of rescuers could see the horror of the children's plight. There were at least fifteen orphans in a large cage in the center of camp. They wept as the evil one taunted them, "You will be my slaves to do my will. When I am done with you, I will feed you to my dogs."

At that declaration, two humongous black dogs, with teeth bared, lunged at the cage as the children screamed.

The evil one laughed. "Storm! Beast! Be patient, my pets. I haven't yet inflicted my terror on these, my newest slaves." He stroked Storm's head and said, "But don't worry. You'll have your chance at them."

The rescuers stared at one another as Mezana shivered. She felt her heart skip a beat. *What if the evil one captures us? This cage and the flashing fangs of the dogs could be our fate.*

But Faith whispered in her ear, "Be strong. They don't have the power to take us."

Beast stretched and sniffed the air, then made a sharp turn in the direction of Asriel's followers and barked ferociously until the evil one roared, "Is someone out there?"

The monstrous dog responded with a low growl as fur rose on the nape of his neck. He took a menacing step toward them, then another.

In a flash, Cara opened the book and whispered, "You are my hiding place and my shield" (Ps. 119:114 GW).

The dog froze, then looked around as if confused before retreating to his master's side.

Faith chuckled under her breath. "We are hidden by Asriel's shield."

"His shield?" Mezana asked.

"It's all around us. Can't you see it?" Faith answered.

Mezana shook her head, but Seth said, "Good work, Cara. They are blind to us. We are now safe to walk into the enemy's camp and rescue the children."

Mezana wasn't so sure, but she was committed to following Asriel's orders. With her heart hammering in her chest, Mezana silently followed Seth and the others as they strolled into the camp. As they passed the dogs, Beast sniffed the air, then put his head on his paws and closed his eyes to sleep.

It was true, Mezana realized. Their band was really hidden by Asriel's shield.

Once at the cage, Seth pulled Asriel's key out of his pocket and quietly unlocked the door.

The children were silent, spellbound at the sight of their rescuers. Mercy held a finger to her lips and said, "We are here to help you, my dears. Please follow us back to the light."

The children nodded, then quietly, in single file, followed Mezana and her friends back to the edge of the woods. Just as they began to step into the dawn of the new day, shouts and howls of fury arose from behind them. A bellowing voice echoed through the treetops. "The orphans have escaped!"

Mezana found herself running into the day with her brave new friends and the orphans. She scooped up a little one into her arms without missing a step. Before she knew it, they were all safe behind her bolted door.

"I'm hungry!" a little voice said. Mezana looked down to see a tiny boy tugging at her sleeve.

Cara opened the book and told the group, "Open your mouth wide, and I will fill it" (Ps. 81:10 GW).

Faith said, "That's good news. I'll check the pantry."

"It's practically bare," Mezana warned.

"Nonsense!" Faith said as she threw the pantry doors open wide. To Mezana's amazement, her pantry was filled with an abundance of food. Enough for everyone! As Mercy set to work preparing breakfast for the children, Seth pulled Mezana and Cara aside.

"We need someone to teach these children the ways of Asriel so they can escape the lies and traps of the evil one."

Cara patted Mezana's arm. "Mezana is a wonderful teacher. She taught me to read and helps me practice with my sword."

Seth looked into Mezana's eyes. "Then, my sister, would you be willing?"

Mezana saw the hope in the little faces around her. She asked Seth, "Do you think this is one of Asriel's purposes for me?"

Before Seth could answer, Cara clapped her hands. "Oh yes! And I will help you!"

Seth smiled as the children cheered. He said, "Then I will have a good report for Asriel. Our rescue mission has been a great success."

The Allegory Explained

This episode shows how our armor goes hand in hand with our giftings to help us achieve our purposes. Take a moment to think about which gifts of the Spirit each of the characters demonstrated: serving, teaching, encouraging, prophesying, preaching, giving, organizing and leading, and using mercy, faith, or knowledge. Combining these gifts with the power of the Word led to victory.

These gifts work the same with us. We each have the leading of the Holy Spirit, and when we combine that with the power of the Word, the gifts of the Spirit, and the armor and weapons described by Paul, we can certainly achieve the purposes God has set for us.

Paul, a Man of Purpose

Paul knew who he was, what he was called to do, and that he was responsible to fulfill his call to God. He explained, "I am an apostle, God's messenger, responsible to no mere man" (1 Cor. 9:1 TLB). We too are responsible to tune our ears to God's call on our lives, whether to encourage, prophesy, teach, preach, serve, give, organize, lead, or offer mercy or comfort. These and other calls are a sacred trust from God, a trust we should take seriously so we can fulfill our purposes.

In *The Purpose Driven Life*, Rick Warren says:

> About thirty years ago, I noticed a little phrase in Acts 13:36 that forever altered the direction of my life. It was only seven words but, like the stamp of a searing hot branding iron, my life was permanently marked by these words: "David served God's purpose in his generation." Now I understood why God called David "a man after my own heart." David dedicated his life to fulfilling God's purposes on earth.[5]

And so must we dedicate our lives to God's purposes, for as Paul taught, "So run your race to win. To win the contest you must deny yourselves many things that would keep you from doing your best. An athlete goes to all this trouble just to win a blue ribbon or a silver cup, but we do it for a heavenly reward that never disappears" (1 Cor. 9:24–25 TLB).

Opening Our Gifts

The Holy Spirit has given gifts to each of us. We know this because Paul explained in 1 Corinthians 12:4–7:

> Now God gives us many kinds of special abilities, but it is the same Holy Spirit who is the source of them all. There are different kinds of service to God, but it is the same Lord we are serving. There are many ways in which God works

in our lives, but it is the same God who does the work in and through all of us who are his. The Holy Spirit displays God's power through each of us as a means of helping the entire church. (TLB)

What are the gifts for? Our gifts enable us to serve God and "to serve one another" (1 Pet. 4:10 NLT).

We've already taken a look at the gifts found in Romans 12, which include prophesying, serving, teaching, preaching, giving, organizing or leading, and mercy. But there are a couple of other passages that list gifts, including 1 Corinthians 12:8–11:

> To one person the Spirit gives the ability to give wise advice; someone else may be especially good at studying and teaching, and this is his gift from the same Spirit. He gives special faith to another, and to someone else the power to heal the sick. He gives power for doing miracles to some, and to others power to prophesy and preach. He gives someone else the power to know whether evil spirits are speaking through those who claim to be giving God's messages—or whether it is really the Spirit of God who is speaking. Still another person is able to speak in languages he never learned; and others, who do not know the language either, are given power to understand what he is saying. It is the same and only Holy Spirit who gives all these gifts and powers, deciding which each one of us should have. (TLB)

Gifts are also listed in 1 Corinthians 12:28:

> Here is a list of some of the parts he has placed in his Church, which is his body:

Apostles,
Prophets—those who preach God's Word,
Teachers,
Those who do miracles,
Those who have the gift of healing,
Those who can help others,
Those who can get others to work together,
Those who speak in languages they have never
    learned. (TLB)

Below, you will find a list of gifts that will help you discern the areas of your purpose. Ask the Lord to give you revelation about your giftings, then check anything that you feel applies to you. Next, put a star by any you feel you may have already used in serving God or others.

_____ Serving: Helping those in physical or spiritual need.

_____ Teaching/preaching: The ability to instruct others about things of God.

_____ Encouraging: Helping others stay on course through correction, affirmation, reassuring, and heartening.

_____ Giving: The ability and vision to meet needs, financially, materially, or spiritually.

_____ Leadership/administration: Guiding and managing others and/or projects.

_____ Mercy: The ability to lessen the suffering or pain of others.

_____ Word of wisdom: The ability to speak truth into lives and situations.

_____ Word of knowledge: The ability to express deeper truths based on deeper revelations.

_____ Faith: A confidence in God and his Word, including a confidence in God's abilities to answer your prayers.

_____ Healing/miracles: Having the faith to pray for miracles and/or for the sick and to see them recover through the power of the Holy Spirit.

_____ Distinguishing (discerning) spirits: The ability to understand whether influences, doctrines, or spirits are of God or Satan.

_____ Prayer: The ability to pray in and through the Holy Spirit.

Using Our Gifts

Pay attention to what you checked, but pay special attention to what you starred, as these may be your strongest gifts. These gifts will give you clues to your purpose. If you are having trouble discerning whether you have a gift, first know that you do. If you are not sure what it is, ask for the opinions of people who love and know you. They may be able to see something in you that you are not yet seeing in yourself.

You may have one, or two, and in some cases, even more gifts, depending on your callings. You may need to pray that any blinders from the enemy will be removed so that you can see what God has given you. And don't discount the Holy Spirit with regard to his creativity. If there is a job that needs to be done and you don't have the particular gifting to do it, God may send someone who has that particular gifting to help. But don't be surprised if God chooses to gift you, if even for a season, so you can perform the job yourself.

There is a secret to using your gifts effectively: be sure to exercise your gifts in love. In 1 Corinthians 13, Paul talks about what the gifts of the Spirit are like when used *without* love:

> I may speak in the languages of humans and of angels. But if I don't have love, I am a loud gong or a clashing cymbal. I may have the gift to speak what God has revealed, and I may understand all mysteries and have all knowledge. I may even have enough faith to move mountains. But if I don't have love, I am nothing. I may even give away all that I have and give up my body to be burned. But if I don't have love, none of these things will help me. (vv. 1–3 GW)

When you use your gifts in love, you will be able to open the supernatural aspects of your gifts. You will be able to combine your service with the love of God.

Romans 12:9–12 says, "Don't just pretend that you love others: really love them. Hate what is wrong. Stand on the side of the good. Love each other with brotherly affection and take delight in honoring each other. Never be lazy in your work, but serve the Lord enthusiastically. Be glad for all God is planning for you. Be patient in trouble, and prayerful always" (TLB).

Stepping into Our Purposes

So what do you do next? You seek God with a prayer like, "Lord, lead me into my purposes." Then you do the next thing

God leads you to do. As the old proverb says, "When you begin to weave, God provides the thread." So weave, live, seek God, and pray, and God will guide you and supply all you need. He may not give you a road map, but he will show you which step to take next.

Here are some additional clues to help you in your journey to purpose. Let's say you realize you have the gift of teaching. Does this mean you need to go to school to get a teaching certificate or rush to seminary to study preaching? Maybe. Ask yourself this question: Knowing I have the gift of teaching, what would I do if I had no fear? The answer to that question could be another hint to your purpose.

Perhaps you answered by saying, "I would teach underprivileged kids how to read." If this idea resonates with you, it could be one of your purposes. But before you do anything life changing, take the idea before the Lord. "Lord, what do you think of this idea? Lead me. Show me if this should be my goal, our vision together. If so, show me the next step to take toward this goal."

Then listen quietly before the Lord. Does your heart leap with joy? Do you hear his affirmation or a divine connection? Or do you feel a disconnect, which is often a no or sometimes a wait.

Then to confirm that you've heard from the Lord, seek additional counsel. Take your quest for purpose to your spouse (if you have one) as well as to your most supportive family members. You may also want to take your quest to your most supportive believing friends. Share your thoughts, then ask your friends and family to help you pray over them. And pray together! You may find that your spouse, friends, and family have some wise counsel and insights to help you discern if this is God's will for you. But you'll also need to use your own discernment as to any counsel you receive and pray about it.

Next, look for passion. Is this idea something you could see yourself doing with enthusiasm? Is it something that would not only fit your skill set but also ignite your motivational drive? For example, just because you have the skill and gifting to teach kids to read doesn't mean you have the passion to do so. A lack of passion or motivation could be a clue that this is not the direction God has planned for you. But at the same time, sometimes motivation and passion are delayed until your calling is met with obedience. Be sure to seek God and follow his lead, especially if your call is not yet clear.

Perhaps as you explore other options you might realize your passion is to homeschool your own kids or to teach your favorite subject at the university level. Or maybe you're called to write training manuals or books, teach Sunday school, or give lectures or training on topics that could make a difference in your field, in your church or community, or in the kingdom. So there's a lot to think about, a lot to pray through.

The next step is to ask God to ignite your heart with vision. But remember, once God gives you your vision of purpose, all you have to do is follow him one step at a time. It's a process that may not happen overnight.

Sometimes God has me follow him on assignments without revealing his purpose until the assignment is complete, and only then do I have that divine aha moment. And sometimes God has me follow him into temporary assignments for only a season. But regardless, God often has me "heaped" in purpose. For example, besides writing books, God has given me the purpose of being a good wife to my husband and a good mother to my kids. He has given me the purpose to lead Christian communicators, publish a Christian women's magazine, reach out to the hurting on social media, and speak to groups and pray for others through the ministry of the prayer team at my church. So my purpose has multiple layers. So does yours.

The most important step to take is the next step. Be open to God's leading and follow it even when you realize the step God has planned for you was not part of your original plan. This is not the time to balk; it's the time to be amazed at what God can do with your life in this generation. As you follow God, it may not be until you look back on your journey that you can see the beautiful tapestry God was creating of your life and finally understand that he had you on assignment all along.

Dear Lord,

Open my eyes so I can see the spiritual gifts you have given me. Please take any blinders off my eyes so I can see what the enemy would try to hide when it comes to my giftings. Please show me how you want me to use the gifts you are revealing. Also reveal your leading, vision, and purposes for my life. Give me the courage to follow your lead, even if only one step at a time. Lord, I give my life to you to serve you and to serve others, whether through my usual job or in a job or vocation you have in mind for me to fulfill. Help me to also serve your purposes in my home, family, church, and community. And give me the gift of love so that your giftings are activated to make a real difference in the circle of influence you are giving me. In Jesus's name, amen.

▬ ARMORED RESPONSE ▬

To help defeat misdirection from your purpose, study, declare, and pray this misdirection-fighting Scripture.

Misdirection-Fighting Scripture

"Work hard to show the results of your salvation, obeying God with deep reverence and fear. For God is working in you, giving you the desire and the power to do what pleases him" (Phil. 2:12–13 NLT).

Declaration to Defeat Misdirection

I thank the Lord that I do not have to earn my salvation. Still, I declare that I will work hard to show the results of what his saving grace has accomplished in my life. I declare that I will obey him with deep reverence and fear, for he is working in me, giving me direction, vision, and power to accomplish the purposes he has planned for me.

Prayer for Victory over Misdirection

Dear Lord,

Thank you for saving me, and thank you that you have purposes planned for my life. I submit myself before you in obedience, asking you to reveal your direction and purposes for me and to give me the power and ability to accomplish all you have prepared in advance for me to accomplish. I choose to obey you in these purposes, knowing that your purposes for me are for good, for life, for serving you and serving others. Thank you that I can follow you into my purposes one step at a time. In Jesus's name, amen.

12

Victory in Jesus

Thank God that he gives us the victory through our Lord
Jesus Christ.

1 Corinthians 15:57 GW

How did I become so familiar with the armor and weapons
of our warfare? Because I have a few battle scars. But the fight
never raged as hot as when I put pen to paper to write this
book. I fought hard, calling on all the weapons, armor, and
mighty name of Jesus so I could win this battle for *my* God-
ordained purpose—to get this message to you.

But my secret weapon was knowing that the battle was
already won. Warren Wiersbe said, "Remember: you are not
fighting *for* victory but *from* victory, for Jesus Christ has already defeated Satan!"[1]

And this is true. In the course of writing this book, I won
one of the biggest battles I've ever fought, starting the night I
began to put my notes and research into my first chapter. As I

Empowered for Purpose

shared earlier, it was that very night my daughter landed in the ICU to fight for her life. I prayed the armor of God over her, and God answered my prayer! Seven days later I was able to bring my daughter home and back to her sweet and happy life.

The reason I knew praying in the armor of God was a powerful prayer was because I'd seen God miraculously answer this same kind of prayer a couple of weeks earlier when I'd led a group of Christian women authors in a time of prayer. Together we

- put on the helmet of salvation—which is Jesus
- put on the breastplate of righteousness—which is Jesus
- put on the belt of truth—which is Jesus
- stood on the gospel of peace—which is Jesus
- took up the shield of faith—which is Jesus
- grabbed hold of the sword of the Spirit—which is Jesus

Then I explained how we are in Jesus and Jesus is in us. I told them that we are seated with him in heavenly places, as Ephesians 2:6 says: "And God raised us up with Christ and seated us with him in the heavenly realms in Christ Jesus." I told them that the enemy is under our feet.

Then we made our victory cry. I held up my hand before them and said, "My little hand is in Jesus's hand." I walked over to Janet, whom I knew to be in great pain, and simply said, "Be healed in Jesus's name."

I walked away, never asking how Janet felt or if Jesus had healed her, and continued my talk on prayer.

180

Janet came to me the next morning with tears in her eyes. "As I was getting ready for bed last night I realized my pain was gone."

"That's wonderful!"

"But you don't know what a miracle this is. My neuropathy was so bad that I wasn't sure I could come to this conference because I wasn't sure I could make it through the airport. Still, I felt compelled to be here. Now I know why. When you said, 'Be healed in the name of Jesus,' Jesus healed me. My pain is completely gone, including the severe pain I had in my knee."[2]

Why did this happen? It happened because of God's grace. God graced us with his gift of healing as we prayed the armor in, through, with, and in agreement with Jesus.

My question is, Who won these battles I've shared?

Jesus! Jesus is the victor of our battles because the battle belongs to him.

In Deuteronomy, Moses explained a few rules of warfare to the Israelites, including, "For the LORD your God is going with you! He will fight for you against your enemies, and he will give you victory!" (20:4 NLT). This warfare strategy explained by Moses is also a good strategy for us whenever we encounter spiritual warfare. God is going with us! He will fight our enemies! He will give us victory!

Our Quest

Paul said, "Thank God that he gives us the victory through our Lord Jesus Christ" (1 Cor. 15:57 GW). This means Jesus will not only empower us in our battle for purpose but also empower us to victory.

Sometimes when I feel discouraged, I remember a time when I was a five-year-old at the county fair. I felt so proud to have my own ticket to the house of mirrors, a maze of mirrors I was sure I could walk through all by myself. But once inside, instead of finding my way out, I continually ran into my own frustrated reflection until I finally burst into tears. I wanted my daddy! I called out to him, and soon I was in his arms, safe and free from my roadblocks.

This is exactly what Jesus does for us. We think we are smart enough to find a way to victory under our own power, but Jesus is our victory and will lead the way out of the maze, past the distractions, lies, and traps of the enemy. He will get us through the thick of the battle if we surrender our trust to him and let him carry us. It's his helmet of salvation that saves us. It's his breastplate of righteousness that protects our hearts. It's his belt of truth that breaks the lies of the enemy. It's his shoes of peace that calm our storms. It's his shield of faith that deflects the fiery darts of the enemy. It's the sword of the Spirit that lights our way through the darkness.

And besides that, he gives us other weapons to help us win our battles, namely, the fruit of the Spirit. Fruit is different from gifts of the Spirit because gifts refer to purposes. Fruit refers to good character empowered by the Holy Spirit. When we walk in the character of Christ as we yield to Christ, we will live in the power of Christ's "love, joy, peace, patience, kindness, goodness, faithfulness, gentleness, and self-control" (Gal. 5:22–23 NLT).

This fruit will not only empower our giftings but also empower us in our purposes, an undefeatable combination!

Mezana's Quest

It had been months since the orphans had been rescued. On this day they sat together on benches beneath the shade of a tree in Mezana's front yard, listening as she taught them about their armor and the purposes of Asriel.

Mezana's heart was inspired by how they took to their lessons, especially as she concluded today's teaching with, "Be sure to keep your armor on, especially if you want to survive the traps set by the evil one."

Mezana looked around at the dear faces, so glad these children had been set free. She closed her lesson plans and said, "I have an exciting announcement. I have just received word from Asriel that he is proud of your progress. He believes that some of you are ready for your first mission. So he has asked me to select a team based on your gifts."

The children looked from one to another expectantly as Mezana continued. "The leader of this team and mission will be Cara," Mezana said as the children clapped. Cara rose and stood by Mezana's side, beaming. "Cara's assistant will be Miles, who also has the gift of leadership. Also, Trent will serve based on his ability to discern truth, and he will be charged to carry the book. Last but not least, Kindra will serve based on her gift of serving others with kindness."

The members of Cara's team rose, and the children clapped while those chosen glowed with joy. But before Mezana released the team to return to their seats, she said, "A warning for us all. I have received word to be on alert for attacks of pride."

Cara asked, "Pride?"

"Pride is what the evil one uses to create division. That way the evil one can hinder our mission as well as separate us one from another," Mezana replied. "When we are split apart or even isolated, the evil one can strip us of effectiveness."

Miles countered, "But we will be wearing our armor."

Mezana put her hand on the boy's shoulder and said, "Armor cannot defend against dark choices you yourself make."

"But *I* would never make a dark choice!" the boy replied as hurt shone from his eyes.

Mezana smiled. "My remark was meant as a caution for us all, Miles."

Trent queried, "How can we defend ourselves against pride?"

"The best cure for pride or dark and willful choices is the fruit of the Spirit."

"You mean our gifts?"

"Your *gifts* are for purpose. *Fruit* is a different but related set of giftings. Fruit develops as we yield our pride. It helps us build good character to help empower our purposes."

After the class was dismissed, an old woman dressed in layers of moldy green pulled Miles aside and whispered into his ear, "I saw how your teacher embarrassed you with her accusations."

Miles looked startled. "What do you mean?"

"Well, it's clear she favors Cara, but in my opinion, you should lead the mission of Asriel."

Miles's eyes widened. "This I already suspected. Thank you for the confirmation."

The old woman clutched his arm and pulled him closer. "Personally, I wouldn't let them get away with any of this. Mezana offended you, then demoted and humiliated you in front of your classmates."

"Now that you mention it, she did keep me from my rightful place as leader of the mission," Miles said, his brow furrowing.

The old woman nodded. "Just trying to be of service, my dear."

"And what is your name?" Miles inquired. "I've not seen you here before."

"That's because I'm a bit of a traveler, dropping by here and there to encourage many, like yourself," the old woman said. "But I'm Mrs. Pickles to you."

Later that afternoon Cara told her teammates, "This is a rescue mission. It turns out there are hungry children down by the Valley of Despair. Asriel has asked us to lead them to the River of Truth, where tables of plenty are being set up for them now."

"I'll take it from here, Cara," Miles said, "considering I'm the natural leader in this group. So is everyone suited up and ready to go?"

Cara blushed. "But the position of leadership has been given to me as *my* responsibility. You are to be my assistant on this mission."

"What Mezana said about me was wrong."

Cara countered, "But Mezana didn't . . ."

"Her very words are the reason I am taking my rightful place." He looked from face to face. "Who is with me?"

Kindra said, "I would be happy to serve either of you."

"Good," Miles exclaimed. "Then you will be on my team."

"Wait a minute. We need to fulfill this mission in unity," Cara said, "or we will become separated and ineffective."

"That's just Mezana's scare tactic," Miles said. "Nothing bad is going to happen. We'll lead the kids to dinner, and that will be that."

Trent said, "I can't put my finger on it, but something about this doesn't seem right."

"I'm trying to make it right," Miles countered. "Truth is one of my giftings too, Trent. As you well know."

With that, Miles started to walk to the Valley of Despair with first Kindra, then Trent, and finally Cara following.

It was Mrs. Pickles who met the team beneath the weeping willows in the heart of the valley. While Miles stopped to greet her, Cara announced to the hungry children who had gathered there, "We've come to take you to a fine meal."

An angry voice interrupted her as a firm hand landed on her shoulder. "Hold on! Cara, you're doing *my* job," Miles exclaimed. "Besides, Mrs. Pickles has a meal set up for the kids just beyond the hill, around the bend and toward the dark woods."

Cara exploded with rage. "Miles, are you too blind to see that this woman is a servant of the evil one?"

Mrs. Pickles let out a wounded cry. "This is what I should expect from a hypocrite as yourself, thinking your way, your food, is better than mine."

Some of the children waiting for their promised meal began to cry, while others began to walk toward the hill Mrs. Pickles had indicated. Miles said to Cara, "See what you have done. You have insulted Mrs. Pickles and frightened the children."

"Wait!" Cara called to the children who had begun to drift away. "Please wait just a little longer and we'll have this confusion cleared up. I promise you."

The children who had started to leave turned as Kindra said, "I no longer know what is true. Do you, Trent?"

"That's why I brought the book," Trent said, pulling it from his knapsack.

Mrs. Pickles hooted a laugh. "That old thing? That's certainly not needed here, not when my banquet is so near."

Trent ignored her as he read the book aloud. "Get rid of all bitterness, rage, anger, harsh words, and slander, as well as all types of evil behavior. Instead, be kind to each other, tenderhearted, forgiving one another, just as God through Christ has forgiven you" (Eph. 4:31–32 NLT).

Kindra began to weep. "I think we've been poisoned with a pride attack!"

Trent turned to Miles. "Can't you see? This was Mezana's warning. Pride leads to dark choices. Pride leads us away from truth."

Miles looked confused. "But Mrs. Pickles said . . ."

Cara interrupted, "What matters is that we follow the words of the book. We need to love one another and ask each other for forgiveness."

Mrs. Pickles folded her arms and warned, "I wouldn't do that, my dearies, not if you want to lead these hungry children to a good meal."

Trent turned to the hag. "But truth lights our way through darkness and confusion, which is exactly what you've created here, Mrs. Pickles."

Cara approached Miles. "I can see that Mezana and I have somehow offended you. Will you forgive us?"

Miles nodded, pleased at the apology until Trent stared him down. "And what do you have to say to Cara, Miles?"

A light dawned in Miles's eyes, and he suddenly looked stricken. "I'm just starting to see what's happened," he said as he turned to Cara. "I'm sorry too. I see now that I was blinded by pride. Will you forgive me, Cara?"

Cara nodded. "Of course."

Miles turned to address Mrs. Pickles but stammered, "Where'd she go?"

Trent explained, "As we were apologizing, Mrs. Pickles just faded away."

Cara turned to the children. "Come with us, kids. We have a wonderful meal for you down by the River of Truth!"

The children cheered. "What are we having?" a bright-eyed boy asked.

Cara chuckled. "It will be a meal that satisfies, and it will be served with love, joy, peace, patience, kindness, goodness, faithfulness, gentleness, and self-control."

"Don't forget victory!" Miles added as the team burst into laughter. And they continued laughing, leading the hungry children all the way to the River of Truth and to a warm meal that filled their bellies with delight.

The Allegory Explained

As with the children, victory is within our grasp. That is, if we can take the blinders off to expose our own pride. As we yield our pride to the Holy Spirit, he plants the fruit of the Spirit in our hearts.

The fruit of the Spirit is our secret weapon. How can the enemy win a battle of worry when we have peace in our hearts? How can the enemy win a battle to divide with anger and jealousy when we forgive and truly love others? How can the enemy win any battle when we are full of joy, patience, kindness, goodness, faithfulness, gentleness, and self-control?

The glad truth is he can't. It's like the apostle James explained:

> Who among you is wise and understanding? Let him show by his good behavior his deeds in the gentleness of wisdom.

But if you have bitter jealousy and selfish ambition in your heart, do not be arrogant and so lie against the truth. This wisdom is not that which comes down from above, but is earthly, natural, demonic. For where jealousy and selfish ambition exist, there is disorder and every evil thing. But the wisdom from above is first pure, then peaceable, gentle, reasonable, full of mercy and good fruits, unwavering, without hypocrisy. And the seed whose fruit is righteousness is sown in peace by those who make peace. (James 3:13–18 NASB)

If we are to have victory in fulfilling our purposes, we each need to respond and then follow our individual God-callings, much like young Gideon, whose story is told in the book of Judges. After receiving a call from the Lord to go to war against the horde of Midianites camped in the valley of Jezreel, Gideon waited on God to confirm his calling, then sent out a call for men to join in the fight. How thrilled he must have been when thirty-two thousand showed up to go to battle with him. But when God complained that Gideon had too many men and should dismiss everyone who was afraid to go into battle, twenty-two thousand men fell out of rank.

Instead of sending the ten thousand men to fight with Gideon, God warned Gideon that there were still too many men in his troop. God directed Gideon to lead his men to a river to drink. He had Gideon dismiss everyone who quenched their thirst by kneeling down to drink from the stream instead of drinking from their cupped hands. That left only three hundred men to defend Gideon's cause. And how do you suppose God equipped these three hundred to fight against the horde of the Midianite army?

God supplied them with four kinds of weapons: an earthen jar, a torch, a ram's horn to blow as a trumpet, and a battle cry.

Let's read how Gideon told his three hundred to use these weapons. "He said to them, 'Keep your eyes on me. When I come to the edge of the camp, do just as I do. As soon as I and those with me blow the rams' horns, blow your horns, too, all around the entire camp, and shout, "For the LORD and for Gideon!"'" (Judg. 7:17–18 NLT).

When the horns blew, the men of Gideon who had hidden their torches inside their jars broke the jars, revealing their torches as their shouts echoed off the valley walls like a roar. "For the LORD and for Gideon!"

What happened next was absolute chaos. The enemy armies of the valley fought as they had never fought before, but the problem was they were fighting one another instead of Gideon's men. Those who weren't killed by their own swordplay were scattered afar. Gideon, through God's leading, won the battle against what seemed like impossible odds!

How do the weapons of Gideon's band of three hundred apply to us? We too are earthen jars, filled with the Spirit of God. When the Spirit breaks forth in our lives, when our hearts are filled with unity with one another, signified by the call of the ram's horn, then all that is left is our battle cry: "For the Lord so that our enemy will know we belong to him!"

Our enemy, the evil one, will flee, and we will have the victory.

Paul's Thorny Warfare Tactic

But still you might be wondering, *What happens when I can't stop the strongman from harassing me?*

I think this was Paul's dilemma when he talked about his "thorn in his flesh" in 2 Corinthians 12:7: "A thorn in the flesh was given to me, a messenger of Satan to buffet me, lest I be exalted above measure" (NKJV).

Many people believe that God sent Paul an illness to keep him from becoming proud. But I'm not sure this is what this passage means. I think the thorn was given to Paul by a messenger of Satan, or a fallen angel, to hinder him and the spread of his message. It is certain that Satan came against Paul and his ministry at every turn, as we learn when Paul talks about his persecutions and infirmities (2 Cor. 12:8–10 NKJV).

Many people believe Paul's infirmity was eye trouble. However, I doubt this because Ananias, through the power of God, had already healed Paul of his eye trouble (blindness) back in Damascus. Also, I doubt that Paul's infirmity was an illness because the Greek word for infirmity is *astheneia*, also meaning "suffering."[3]

And how Paul *suffered* for the cause of Christ! Take a look at the sufferings Paul listed just prior to his "thorn in the flesh" passage.

> I have worked harder, been put in prison more often, been whipped times without number, and faced death again and again. Five different times the Jewish leaders gave me thirty-nine lashes. Three times I was beaten with rods. Once I was stoned. Three times I was shipwrecked. Once I spent a whole night and a day adrift at sea. I have traveled on many long journeys. I have faced danger from rivers and from robbers. I have faced danger from my own people, the Jews, as well as from the Gentiles. I have faced danger in the cities, in the deserts, and on the seas. And I have faced danger from

men who claim to be believers but are not. I have worked hard and long, enduring many sleepless nights. I have been hungry and thirsty and have often gone without food. I have shivered in the cold, without enough clothing to keep me warm. (2 Cor. 11:23–27 NLT)

Wow! I think suffering through persecution was indeed Paul's thorn.

How did God answer Paul's request to remove this thorn? God told Paul, "My grace is sufficient for you, for My strength is made perfect in weakness" (2 Cor. 12:9 NKJV).

You mean God didn't offer *relief* from Paul's sufferings, only *grace*? Yes, and Paul's reaction was priceless. He said, "Therefore most gladly I will rather boast in my infirmities, that the power of Christ may rest upon me. Therefore I take pleasure in infirmities, in reproaches, in needs, in persecutions, in distresses, for Christ's sake. For when I am weak, then I am strong" (2 Cor. 12:9–10 NKJV).

Why am I sharing this passage about suffering in a chapter about victory? Because Paul's weaknesses, combined with God's grace, caused the strongman to be defeated. We know this is true because Paul's writings were copied and spread among the churches of his day. Since then his writings have continued to spread around the world for the past two thousand years. Today you can find Paul's writings nestled within a collection of books we know as the New Testament of Jesus Christ, read by throngs of people. Not a bad victory I'd say.

Paul's tactic of long-suffering, combined with God's grace, turned out to be tactical spiritual warfare. It's not the kind of tactic one would expect to win a war. But as Paul said in 2 Corinthians 10:3–5:

It is true, we live in a body of flesh. But we do not fight like people of the world. We do not use those things to fight with that the world uses. We use the things God gives to fight with and they have power. Those things God gives to fight with destroy the strong-places of the devil. We break down every thought and proud thing that puts itself up against the wisdom of God. We take hold of every thought and make it obey Christ. (NLV)

And as I mentioned earlier, the Holy Spirit gives us weapons against which there is no law. "But the Holy Spirit produces this kind of fruit in our lives: love, joy, peace, patience, kindness, goodness, faithfulness, gentleness, and self-control" (Gal. 5:22–23 NLT). And Jesus himself told us, "You didn't choose me. I chose you. I appointed you to go and produce lasting fruit, so that the Father will give you whatever you ask for, using my name" (John 15:16 NLT).

Putting It All Together

We have studied how to find, defend, and ignite our purposes through the weapons of our warfare: the armor of God, the gifts and fruit of the Spirit, the indwelling of the Holy Spirit, the power of the name of Jesus, the Word of God, and our battle cries and prayers for victory.

Like Gideon, we have learned how to let our light, which is the Holy Spirit, shine into our daily battles.

We also know that though there are times when the battle is hard and times when the fight may be long, we can rest in the peace of the Lord. Paul instructs us in 1 Timothy 6:12,

"Fight the good fight of faith. Take hold of the life that lasts forever. You were chosen to receive it" (NLV).

There will be a day when we will cease our fighting, complete our missions, and finally fulfill all our purposes, and on that day we will lay down our weapons to hear the Lord say, "Well done, good and faithful servant!" (Matt. 25:21).

But until that day, stay strong and remember that Jesus said, "You didn't choose me. I chose you. I appointed you to go and produce lasting fruit, so that the Father will give you whatever you ask for, using my name" (John 15:16 NLT).

Dear Lord,

Thank you for choosing me! Thank you for appointing me to go and produce lasting fruit. Thank you that you will give me whatever I ask when I come to you in Jesus's name.

Thank you too for my purposes! Walk with me to fulfill them and teach me how to fight the enemy wrapped in your armor and with love, joy, peace, patience, kindness, goodness, faithfulness, gentleness, and self-control. The enemy cannot defeat these weapons. Thank you that the light of your Word and Spirit is shining through me and into the darkness. Thank you that you have already won the war. In Jesus's name, amen.

ARMORED RESPONSE

Our best weapon against the enemy is the power of Christ. Spend a moment enjoying God's truth that we win!

Victory Scripture

"We thank God for the power Christ has given us. He leads us and makes us win in everything. He speaks through us wherever we go. The Good News is like a sweet smell to those who hear it" (2 Cor. 2:14 NLV).

Declaration of Victory

Thank God that I have received Christ's power in me, for he has made me a victor, winning in everything. He speaks to me wherever I am. He lets me share the Good News so that it is a sweet aroma to all who hear my message. I am a victor in and through Christ.

Prayer for Victory

Dear Lord,

Thank you that the power of Christ is in me, guiding me, leading me to share the Good News and to fulfill the purposes he has set for me. Thank you that in him I can win every battle and accomplish the callings you have on my life. I celebrate you, God. And I honor my victor, Jesus Christ, who made my victories possible through his work on the cross. Because of his work, I am victorious, as he has already won the war.

I pray this in your armor, in and through and with and in agreement with you. I pray this with the Holy Spirit inside of me. I pray this through the power of your Word and in the power of the name and the blood of Jesus. Amen.

In conclusion, let's end with Ephesians 6:10: "A final word: Be strong in the Lord and in his mighty power" (NLT).

Notes

Introduction

1. Sanford F. Bennett, "In the Sweet By and By," 1868.

2. Rick Stedman, *Praying the Armor of God: Trusting God to Protect You and the People You Love* (Eugene, OR: Harvest House, 2015), 28.

3. Susie Larson, *Your Beautiful Purpose: Discovering and Enjoying What God Can Do through You* (Minneapolis: Bethany, 2013), 20.

Chapter 1 Our Quest for Purpose

1. Louis and Katherine L'Amour, *War Party* (New York: Bantom Books, 1975), 7.

2. Charles F. Stanley, *God Has a Plan for Your Life: The Discovery That Makes All the Difference* (Nashville: Thomas Nelson, 2008), 13.

3. Ibid.

4. Lysa M. TerKeurst, *Living Life on Purpose: Discovering God's Best for Your Life* (Chicago: Moody, 2000), 176.

Chapter 2 Who Are You Wearing?

1. Saundra Dalton-Smith, "7 Ways to Disarm Disappointment," *Leading Hearts*, July/August 2015, 35.

2. David Wilkerson, "Seated with Jesus," December 28, 2009, *David Wilkerson Today Blogspot*, http://davidwilkersontoday.blogspot.com/2009/12/seated-with-jesus.html.

3. TerKeurst, *Living Life on Purpose*, 178.

Chapter 3 Wearing the Truth of Christ

1. Carly's story used with permission.

2. Stedman, *Praying the Armor of God*, 27–28.

3. Mark I. Bubeck, *Overcoming the Adversary: Warfare Praying against Demon Activity* (Chicago: Moody, 1984), 71.

4. Ann's story used with permission.

Chapter 4 Wearing the Righteousness of Christ

1. "'Ambushed' Officer: God Told Me to Put on Bulletproof Vest," *USA Today*, August 3, 2015, http://www.sltrib.com/home/2798877-155/am bushed-officer-god-told-me-to.

2. Stedman, *Praying the Armor of God*, 32.

3. Neil T. Anderson, *The Daily Discipler: Daily Readings That Will Give You a Solid Foundation* (Ventura, CA: Regal Books, 2005), 484.

Chapter 5 Walking in the Gospel of Peace

1. Max Anders, *New Christian's Handbook* (Nashville: Thomas Nelson, 1999), 134.

2. Warren W. Wiersbe, *Ephesians through Revelation*, vol. 2 (Colorado Springs: David C. Cook, 2001), 57.

3. Ibid.

4. Lloyd John Ogilvie, *Experiencing the Power of the Holy Spirit* (Eugene, OR: Harvest House, 2001), 131.

5. Ibid.

6. TerKeurst, *Living Life on Purpose*, 176.

Chapter 6 Wielding the Shield of Faith

1. J. Dwight Pentecost, *Designed to Be Like Him: God's Plan for Fellowship, Conduct, Conflict, and Maturity* (Grand Rapids: Kregel, 1966), 249.

2. Thelma Wells, *Don't Give In . . . God Wants You to Win!* (Eugene, OR: Harvest House, 2009), 195–96.

3. Kay Arthur, *Lord, Is It Warfare? Teach Me to Stand: A Devotional Study on Spiritual Victory* (Colorado Springs: Waterbrook Press, 2000), 249.

4. Wells, *Don't Give In . . . God Wants You to Win!*, 195.

Chapter 7 Wearing the Helmet of Salvation

1. Based on an interview with Dianne Butts. Used with permission.
2. Mark Batterson, *The Grave Robber* (Grand Rapids: Baker, 2014), 263. Batterson also notes, "Thanks to Martin Luther for this thought. He said, 'Preach as if Jesus was crucified yesterday, rose from the dead today and is coming back tomorrow.'"
3. Charles Spurgeon, *Spurgeon's Sermons on Prayer* (Peabody, MA: Hendrickson, 2007), 412.
4. Ibid., 412.
5. Pentecost, *Designed to Be Like Him*, 251.
6. Scott Adams, *Dilbert* comic strip, August 19, 2015; August 20, 2015; August 21, 2015; distributed by Universal Uclick, www.dilbert.com.
7. Pat Williams, *The Warrior Within* (Ventura, CA: Regal Books/Gospel Light, 2009), 134.
8. Charles F. Stanley, *When the Enemy Strikes: The Keys to Winning Your Spiritual Battles* (Nashville: Thomas Nelson, 2004), 166.
9. Ibid.

Chapter 8 Brandishing the Sword of the Spirit

1. Based on an interview with Roxanne Max. Used with permission.
2. TerKeurst, *Living Life on Purpose*, 44.
3. Andrew Murray, *The Spiritual Life* (Washington, PA: CLC Publications, 2013), online edition.
4. Charles F. Stanley, *The Wonderful Spirit-Filled Life* (Nashville: Thomas Nelson, 1994), 39.
5. Ibid., 41.

Chapter 9 Praying on All Occasions

1. Based on Linda Evans Shepherd, "Even the Winds Obey," *Leading Hearts*, July/August 2015, 3.
2. Andrew Murray, *Power in Prayer: Classic Devotions to Inspire and Deepen Your Prayer Life* (Bloomington, MN: Bethany, 2011), 15.
3. *Strong's Concordance of the Bible* (Peabody, MA: Hendrickson, 2007), Lexicon, G89.
4. Cheri Fuller and Jennifer Kennedy Dean, *The One Year Praying the Promises of God* (Carol Stream, IL: Tyndale, 2012), 104.
5. Ibid.

Chapter 10 Defeating the Strongman

1. For more information on breaking free of organizations that worship Greek and other gods, download a free prayer at http://bit.ly/1NeMbrS.

2. Based on an anonymous interview.

3. Bubeck, *Overcoming the Adversary*, 14.

4. Lawrence O. Richards, *The Full Armor of God: Defending Your Life from Satan's Schemes* (Grand Rapids: Chosen, 2013), 65.

5. C. H. Spurgeon, *Satanic Hindrances*, vol. 11, sermon #657, http://www.spurgeongems.org/vols10-12/chs657.pdf.

6. Ibid.

Chapter 11 Breakthrough to Your Purpose

1. Charles F. Stanley, *Success God's Way: Achieving True Contentment and Purpose* (Nashville: Thomas Nelson, 2000), 183–84.

2. Max Lucado, *Traveling Light: Releasing the Burdens You Were Never Intended to Bear* (Nashville: Thomas Nelson, 2001), 49.

3. Ibid., 48.

4. Ibid., 48–49.

5. Rick Warren, *The Purpose Driven Life* (Grand Rapids: Zondervan, 2012), day 40.

Chapter 12 Victory in Jesus

1. Warren W. Wiersbe, *The Strategy of Satan* (Eugene, OR: Tyndale, 1979), x–xi.

2. Janet's story used with permission.

3. http://biblehub.com/greek/769.htm.

Linda Evans Shepherd has been married to Paul for over thirty years and is the mother of two.

She is a bestselling and multiple-award-winning author of over thirty books, including *When You Don't Know What to Pray, Called to Pray, The Stress Cure, Praying through Hard Times*, and the Potluck Club series.

Besides writing books, Linda shares her heart with groups around the United States, Canada, and Europe. For more information about her speaking ministry, go to www.Got ToPray.com.

Linda is also the president of Right to the Heart ministries with the following outreaches:

- *Leading Hearts* magazine: get a free copy at Leading Hearts.com
- AWSA (Advanced Writers and Speakers Association): AWSA.com
- The God Test project: GodTest.com
- Suicide prevention help: ThinkingAboutSuicide.com
- Instant Writers Conference: InstantWritersConference .com

You may follow Linda on:

- Twitter: @LindaShepherd and @MyLeadingHearts
- Facebook: www.facebook.com/linda.e.shepherd
- *Leading Hearts* magazine's Facebook: www.facebook .com/leadingheartsmag
- Pinterest: www.pinterest.com/abigheart/

Go to GotToPray.com for free prayer resources.

How to Bring Your Burdens to God –And Expect Answers

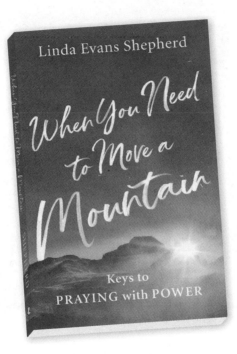

In this practical and encouraging book, quickly find the specific help you need to pray for the things close to your heart. You'll also learn how to develop your own intercessory prayer battle strategy and to celebrate each victory with thanksgiving.

PRAYER CHANGES THINGS.
PRAYING GOD'S PROMISES
CHANGES *EVERYTHING*.

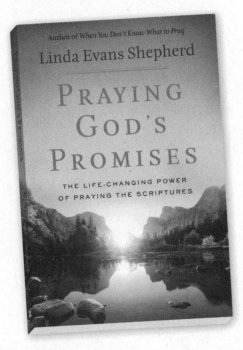

In this inspiring book, Linda Evans Shepherd reveals that God's will is not a mystery—it's clearly laid out in his Word through his many promises. Through stories, practical application, examples of prayers, and guided reflection, she leads you toward a more powerful prayer life. Arranged by topic for ease of use, this book shows you how to pray God's promises of peace, for health, for relationships, for your children, and so much more.